First published in the United States of America in 2025
by Rizzoli International Publications, Inc.
49 West 27th Street
New York, NY 10001
www.rizzoliusa.com

Copyright © Mary Randolph Carter
Photography: Carter Berg
Watercolor illustrations: Cary Carter Turpin

Publisher: Charles Miers
Editor: Ellen Nidy
Design: Aoife Wasser
Production Manager: Maria Pia Gramaglia
Managing Editor: Lynn Scrabis

ISBN: 978-0-8478-4398-5
Library of Congress Control Number: 2025436719

Printed in China
2025 2026 2027 2028 / 10 9 8 7 6 5 4 3 2 1

Visit us online:
Instagram.com/RizzoliBooks
Facebook.com/RizzoliNewYork
X: @Rizzoli_Books
Youtube.com/user/RizzoliNY

LIVE WITH THE THINGS YOU LOVE

LIVE WITH THE THINGS YOU LOVE

...and you'll live happily ever after

MARY RANDOLPH CARTER

Photography by Carter Berg

RIZZOLI
NEW YORK

New York · Paris · London · Milan

CONTENTS

INTRODUCTION

I recently rewatched *Nomadland*, the 2020 drama film about a woman named Fern who later in life embarks on a journey in an old van packed with a few essentials. I thought maybe one day I'll do what she did. I'll get rid of all my possessions, except a few things that really matter, pack them into a vintage airstream and take to the road.

You laugh because many of you know how much I love my stuff and how I'm known as a collector/junker and letting go of all the things I've collected for my seven decades (who's counting?) on this earth would be astounding and anathema to who I am and how I've lived. But maybe *astounding* is what we are ultimately looking for and how we want to live our lives, not just at the end, but every day, and right from the beginning.

What makes life *astounding*, I think, is not the things we've collected and lived with but the people and the memories we associate with them. We cling to those things that connect us to those people and the stories that emanate from them. They are the things we want to live with because they give character, meaning, warmth, and a personal kind of beauty to the places we call Home.

Truthfully, I've not had that many homes.

(I've never been a nomad, except for the years after two fires uprooted our family when I was ten and sixteen). My life has been dug deep into just a few places: my childhood bedroom on the third floor of our family's home on Monument Avenue in Richmond, Virginia; a room above our storage house at River Barn in Virginia's Tidewater area; my private lair in the basement of the seventeenth-century house we moved to later; a fifth-floor studio apartment when I started life on my own in New York City, the apartment I've shared for almost five decades with my husband and our two sons, with a view of the treetops of Central Park and the rooftop of the Metropolitan Museum; and finally, the country home in Upstate New York that sheltered us during the pandemic and is our refuge on weekends and holidays.

I once read that every single object has a god inside, and that's why we cherish them. I believe that. And I would add that each object in our homes—passed on, gifted, or collected—also has a story that reveals not only how it came to be and how it came to us, but how it shares who we are and where we've been. Taken together these collections of things create the memory and personality of the places we call home.

Yep, that's me surrounded by a crazy collection, of things I've collected over the years. Thomas Jefferson once wrote, "That which we elect to surround ourselves with becomes the museum of our souls and the archive of our experiences." I doubt my plastic chicken, paint-by-numbers poodle, my wooden daisy handbag, or my hand-knitted doll would have been the objects he might have elected to surround himself with, and yet these are some of the things that are the "museum of my soul" that I couldn't live without.

So, what are the things I've carried with me from home to home so far, and what are the things I would take on my pared-down journey—the things that matter, the things that last? On my desk a yellow poodle lamp sheds light on a village of my personal objects—a small metal statue of George Washington (see him close-up on the following page) flaking paint and lassoed with a red tag bearing a handwritten message To DAD love American Junk; a pair of primitive pottery vessels, one turquoise and one brown, made for me by my young sons long ago; an iron green frog weighing down a pile of postcards; a framed love letter from my mother—Dearest Howard, Tippy, Carter, Sam, I love you—Pat.

During the pandemic, like a lot of us, tethered to our homes, I spent a lot of time revisiting the things I have collected and lived with for over five decades in this apartment. What I discovered was the joy certain objects have brought to me and my family and the character they have added to the way we have lived. Walking through our rooms I focused on the things that brought them to life, things that seemed to have always been there, that told a story preserving a certain sense of familiarity, of memory, of recognition that this is indeed our home. They are the things our sons gravitate to when they visit, like the dancing Pierrot music box still standing in the little cabinet of their childhood treasures in what had been their old bedroom. They wind it up and, in that moment, listening to the tinkling tune, they are happily reassured that this was and still is their home sweet home.

Live with the things you love, and you'll live happily ever after. That is my mantra and the title of this book. Throughout its pages I will share with you the things I have lived with in our apartment in the city and our house in the country that for so many years have brought me and my family a special kind of happiness. They are my personal totems—a funny concrete mushroom, silly garden elves, a raggedy bear rocking chair, the piano that belonged to Howard's mother that our grandchildren love to bang on now. Each of us cherishes the beauty of different things that tell different stories, and so I visited the homes and getaways of many old friends who have shared the things and lessons learned that have made their living special and each of their homes distinctive and joyful.

I once heard an old hymn sung whose message seems at the core of all of this—

Where your treasure is, there your heart shall be.
All that you possess will never set you free.
Seek the things that last; come and learn from me.
Where your treasure is, your heart shall be.

Nope, I'm not packing up a van. I'm not becoming a nomad. Everything I need to make me happy is right here around me. Turn the page and follow along.

My desk, an old farm table, tucked into the back of the living room in our apartment (see pages 20 and 21) is cluttered on top with so many things like the statue of George Washington (can you find it?), and above it is an exhibit of flea market paintings surrounding a little red and white cabinet with my initials painted on it and a mysterious red hand-pointing at the oval portrait of a ballerina, and down under wobbly stacks of some of my favorite books.

Believe it or not, this vintage French provincial cane-backed dining chair is my desk chair—totally impractical and totally not my style, but when I spotted it and a twin in a favorite junk haunt in Hudson, New York, the absurdity of their bright yellow color pulled at my collector's heartstrings! I accessorized this one with my antique hand-painted western-styled vest and a cushion covered with a piece from a faded Indian print bed spread. Now, it feels like mine!

This little statue of George Washington (actually an iron bank) sat on my father's office desk for years. He never removed the little red tag reminding him it was a gift from American Junk, the antique shop (sort of) that my sister Nell and I opened around the corner. My father, a Virginian, was a lover of American history and so this slightly battered figure of our first president given to him by his daughters made him very happy. After he passed away, I decided to bring George home to my desk in New York City. Whenever I glance at him, I think of what a happy companion he was to my father on his desk, and I smile.

Things that I love at Elm Glen Farm, our country getaway, presiding over a flaking blue-painted metal garden table are a little clay girl wearing around her neck a red-threaded bracelet that says, "Merci," a souvenir from the Parisian store by the same name, a drippy candelabra holding different colored tapers, a little woodpecker that picks up toothpicks stored in the log, a pink glass ashtray that was my grandmother's, and beautifully battered books discovered (with many more) at Rodgers Book Barn in Hillsdale, New York. The painted tin vase displaying the hydrangeas has a hole in it, so I store a jar inside to hold the water. The vintage cookie tin stores a supply of votive candles.

15

Mary Randolph Carter

LIVING with TOO MUCH STUFF

I'm not good with change. We, my husband, Howard, and I have lived in our apartment twelve stories up with a view of the treetops of Central Park and the roof of the Metropolitan Museum of Art for over five decades. Never once did we consider moving. Oh, take that back! There was one time when our two boys were young and rambunctious that we thought about moving out of the city, finding a house, and commuting back and forth to our jobs in Manhattan. As an experiment we took a train to a town 45 minutes out of the city and halfway there decided the commuting life was not for us. So, here we are—the two of us (our boys, now men, moved out long ago)—living as we have for all these years surrounded by the things we have collected, been gifted, cherished, and tripped over packed into these sun-filled, lived-in five rooms. It is our home.

Look around and you will see the things that we have lived with and loved. There's the slightly tarnished pewter collection of plates, bowls and goblets, a wedding gift from my mother and father, shining out of the big pine cupboard. It was a gift from Howard that took over a living room wall that I always dreamed of as a spot for a fireplace, but now with the sun reflecting off it warms the room just as well. On the chest of drawers, starting left, are a marble Buddha, a pink doll's chair standing guard along with a pink metal bloom on either side of a pine lockbox filled with homeless detritus, and a pair of carved wooden animals (with very long tails) atop a round Shaker-style pantry box. The paintings of the horse and the cow on the wall followed me home from a favorite London flea market. An auricula blooms above them. I have always thought it to be the most romantic flower but have never actually grown one.

Previous page: Bardot, my vintage French elephant, oversees a vignette of loved things in our living room: a childhood portrait of me in a blue velvet dress, and our Lady of Guadeloupe. On the old English cricket table that's home to a wire basket of marble grapes, a long-eared stone jackrabbit, and a stacked tower of old books. When I'm not wearing the romantic hand-painted cowgirl vest, it clothes the yellow French-style cane-backed chair.

Following pages: To create a cozy area for my desk at the end of our long living room and to allow the sun to stream through, I crafted a wobbly open partition of five driftwood pine posts, now decorated with fringed flag bunting, hanging fish decoys, and an old watermelon sign. The colorful Mexican lantern suspended from the ceiling, lit at twilight with battery-operated votives, is for romantic ambiance.

"The things I can't live without are always tied to my family."

Mary Randolph Carter

Clockwise from top left: We grew up with Saint Bernards, and this vintage portrait was a present to my father, who loved them so much, and a reminder to the nine of us children who were cared for by them like Nana, who watched over the Darling siblings in Peter Pan. This little orange-and-green-glazed cup and saucer made by our younger son Sam when he was six alwasy deserves a place of honor. My husband, Howard, always asked my mother if he could have her beautifully tarnished Junior Championship golf trophy from 1937 and she always said, "One day." In our kitchen now, we look at it every morning and think of her club in hand.

Opposite: *Found in a junk shop on the Outer Banks of North Carolina, we call this our "Jasper Johns Chair," an old Adirondack scraped down to so many layers of paint it reminded us of the work of that great American painter. Turns out he actually stayed in the same hotel there we enjoyed for so many summers. Imagine!*

Clockwise from left: Perfectly sized for our sons when they were young, these two little chairs still accommodate children (and every so often a grown-up—yikes!) in our living room today. A 17 ½" rustic folk art wooden carving captures the elegant form of our sixteenth president Abraham Lincoln—all six foot four of him—standing book in hand. An Easter present to my mother, this giant wooden rabbit crouched for years in our family home in Virginia, now she crouches in our living room (page 20). I love Charles Dickens but this is one of his classics I will never page through thanks to artist Leanne Shapton's strikingly realistic hand-painted wooden interpretation.

Wooden fish swim happily around a bleached cow skull displayed on the trapstake partition that divides our long living room, yet allows the light to shine through. The crumbling nun, prayed for many years in my family home in Virginia. She now keeps watch over ours moving from place to place.

I was a young wife and mother-to-be when we moved into 12D. We had lived a few blocks away in a smaller apartment when we first married. It was the New York City apartment I had always dreamed of—a charming brownstone with a working fireplace, a tiny kitchen, and a cozy bedroom. Though practicality wasn't exactly our thing, with a child coming we decided we might look for something larger. Luckily, we had good friends who told us about an apartment in the building they were living in—12D! We moved in with the things we had furnished that first apartment with, but, sadly our handcrafted bed constructed of pine driftwood posts didn't make it (too wobbly), so my father built us a rustic facsimile. An old worn floorboard became the sturdy headboard secured on either end by a pair of driftwood posts like the ones in our living room partition, and salvaged from our original bed. (See a smidgen of one opposite strung with a faded construction paper chain and a picture of my mom and dad balanced on the ledge next to it.)

In the little space between my side of the bed opposite and the towering green storage cupboard(see following pages), is my personal altar of sacred objects. I have carefully placed them there over the years as totems of comfort and security to protect my nights from anxiety and restless slumber. (No sleeping potions for me!) When the lights go out (a funny yellow wooden lamp with a green tin shade), my old black rosary beads nestled at its base are just a reach a way. The giant wooden pair dangling from a portrait of St. Theresa belonged to my great aunt Liza and were a Christmas gift from my sister Liza who was named after her. On the shelf to their left is a blue plastic holy water receptacle in the image of the Blessed Mother. Below the shelf is a faded tin ex-voto of a young boy kneeling in thankful prayer to the Blessed Mother for saving his life from a tragic fall. Below that it is a romantic photograph of Howard's mother as a young girl, and to its left are more modern photographs of me with my infant son Sam. The oil painting leaning on the wooden cabinet between a basket of cushy clothes and stacks of comforting books reminds me of a heroine from a Virginia Woolf novel.

Previous page: If you turn to page 32 you will see reflected in the mirror the two giant birds in this grand collage by artist Tom Judd that dominate our hallway exhibiton. Surrounding it is a collection of original thrift shop art and paint-by-numbers tulips. The old English settle, softened by a mix of gingham pillows and a well-dented cushion, is a daily destination for tying on or kicking off sneakers.

Clockwise from above: A wooden carving of a mother embracing her two sons reminds me of me and my boys. A shelf of miniature books and tiny objects, like the green teapot, candlestick, wooden pony, and white swan, are protected above by a sacred assembly of miniature saints. A close-up of the giant wooden rosary dangling (seen on the previous page) was a gift from my sister Liza; Before they moved in with us, this chummy pair of Ralph Lauren Polo bears, a gift to my father, lived in Virginia, where presumably the moth holes originated.

Opposite: *A peeling green cupboard stores wardrobe essentials—socks, scarves, and underwear, as well as the open precious collections of books, favorite saints, a wire birdcage, and paintings. A blue painting by my mother tucked behind St. Theresa standing her ground on a wooden box decorated with red florets.*

The first thing you see when you enter the world of 12D is a giant wooden dough bowl filled with a cargo of metal painted bananas. Howard gave them to me so long ago that neither one of us can remember why or when or where he could possibly have discovered them. For sure they send a message to all that enter—"Do not take this home too seriously! Just come on in and have fun, fun, fun!" They are so heavy that once they found a home on that long wooden table in our hallway they've never wandered. The handmade wooden violin above is another fake—a stage prop of some sort. The pair of framed .mirrors, one of which reflects a pair of huge birds in a painting by my friend Tom Judd, were a housewarming present from my mother and father. I smeared red paint on the plastic battery-operated candles to give them a little life. The large rusty lantern is lit every night in homage to the distressed statue of an unknown saintly woman in prayer who stood for years next to a fireplace at Muskettoe Pointe Farm, our family home in Virginia. That was where we grew up with hordes of Saint Bernards, and because my father loved them so, I was always giving him vintage portraits of them, like the one crouching under the violin.

Sharon & Paul Mrozinski

LIVING
with
LOVE

My mother and I traveled together through the books that we loved. We had never been to Maine, but once we read Sarah Orne Jewett's *The Country Of The Pointed Firs*, we could never go there. The real Maine could never be as good as "the shores of the pointed firs" and the "white clapboarded little town" of Dunnet that the writer took us to, but somehow when I traveled many years later with my son, Carter, to Vinalhaven, Maine, to tell the story of Sharon and Paul Mrozinski, I thought perhaps I had been mistaken.

If you believe in true love, then read on. When Sharon and Paul first met in September 1977 they were married, but not to each other. Sharon lived in Carmel Valley, California, and had contacted Paul, an architect, to work on a project. According to Paul, "that project turned into a life's project." Or as Sharon puts it, "a life's solution." In other words, they fell in love.

Sharon had moved from Arizona, where she was raised, and came to California in her twenties. Paul, who grew up on the south side of Chicago, moved to Monterey in 1971 after his last duty station in the army at Fort Ord. He took a job with an architectural firm and in 1976 opened his own. In 1983, having both departed their marriages, they celebrated New Year's Eve in Paris. They stayed for a month and in 1987, having decided to move to Maine where they had purchased an old sea captain's house in Wiscasset, they invited their friends to a going-away party that turned into a wedding. This was ten years after they had met and all four of their children were there—her two sons and Paul's two daughters.

They opened their shop on the ground floor and name it The Marston House after the family that had lived there for years. After eighteen months of refurbishing it, Paul continued his architectural practice with a firm in Portland. But five years later, tired of that drive back and forth, he resigned, parked his car, and found an easier commute—right across the street. Treats was a little store run by a friend specializing in local products—coffee, cheese, wine, and candy. When she decided to sell, they jumped at the chance. For fourteen years Paul could wave to Sharon as she ran Marston House and he expanded Treat's size and offerings. In 2006, after the the two of them had committed to a healthier way of living and diet, they decided to sell it. Paul says, "I just couldn't do it anymore—selling things filled with sugar that we no longer believed in." That's when they started living in France six months of the year.

Since 1999, they had been traveling to France to buy French homespun peasant fabrics for their American clientele and ended up making French furnishings and inventory their total specialty. Their first purchase was in the village of Bonnieux, and, then having extended their buying trips, they bought an apartment on a hill in the village. In 2016, when they decided they were ready to leave Wiscasset fulltime, they offered Marston House to one of their children. When that didn't work out, deciding where to live next was easy for Sharon—France, of course! Less so for Paul. Sharon's original dream of Maine now belonged to both of them.

That summer, renting a cottage in Vinalhaven, an island only accessible by an hour's ferry ride from the mainland, they spotted a wreck of a house on Main Street that had once been a shop. They decided to look at it, and when Paul walked in, he says, "I saw the whole thing." The decision was made. They would have the best of the two worlds they both loved—France and Maine. Two months after they'd first seen it, what would become Marston House Vinalhaven on Main Street was their shop and their home.

Previous page: For Sharon and Paul the colors of their life in Maine are all shades of blue like this window display at The Marston House Vinalhaven.
Clockwise from top left: Paul and Sharon share a sunset hug. A weathered table set for dinner on the second-story deck. My beloved copy of The Country of the Pointed Firs, 1896, my Maine lodestar. A sailboat glides by a familiar tree-lined landscape of Maine; Sharon welcomes guests to the front door of Marston House.

When Sharon and Paul had their store in Wiscasset, the artist Jamie Wyeth would stop by often. He was greatly absorbed by a scarecrow crow in the backyard dressed in bib overalls and a flannel shirt. One day he asked if he might buy it. Sharon had to decline as it was a parting gift from her two best friends when she left Carmel Valley. When he told her he would like to paint it she told him to take it and bring it back when he was finished. It was Christmas four years later when he brought it back, along with the gift of a watercolor study for the painting. Today it hangs above another crow made of tar paper bought years ago in Maine. The candle holder is an early French hog scraper made of tin, and according to Sharon, it tilts from its use lighting the way in French caves used to store wine under ancient homes. When she discovered a collection of her prized beeswax candles stored in a firkin(a small cask) in her kitchen had bent from the sun she was delighted and chose one to live in the wobbly candlestick holder in her land of crows.

Top: An old teak garden chair with a vintage Panama hat, each found in France years ago, face Vinalhaven's Main Street. It's Sharon's private vantage point to quietly observe what's going on. She calls it her "crow's nest."

Below: An old handmade cardboard box topped with an antique photo was a gift from a friend. The fish carved from bone on a string was left one day in the shop. Somehow, they ended up together.

Opposite: Something to crow about—Jamie Wyeth's watercolor study of a scarecrow crow and a feathered relative made of tar paper snared in Maine. "If only we had bought more," says Sharon.

Previous pages: In their cozy living quarters on the second floor above the shop, everything's painted white—including beadboard walls and rustic beamed ceilings. Moving into a much smaller space the couple had to figure out which pieces worked. Sharon's white sofa was the perfect scale. When it's just the two of them they eat right there on the coffee table. Larger groups gather at the long table in the back of the room. All these pieces have served different purposes in their homes for almost five decades.

Following pages: Though she never thought of herself as a collector, Sharon will admit to one or two. The first being the pears on the mantlepiece and huddled together in the wooden shelf to its right, and the second being wooden hands. That started when she and a good friend discovered a pair and decided that each should own one—"symbolic of our friendship," Sharon says. The ladder leaning to the left leads to up to an attic space where their kids and grandkids as well as friends sleep. Though, there's a full bathroom and shower, it's a little like camping on old L.L. Bean cots.

Sharon says "I love pears, the shape of them, their colors—they remind me of human bodies. I started picking them up during that
stone fruit era—one by one. Then Paul would get one for me and then
the kids. Once you've started a collection, people love to add to it. There
are the pears themselves—all different sizes, picture of pears, and the
clockface with pears on our mantelpiece. We even planted them in
our garden."

Finding unusual lamps is such a challenge. Sharon found this winner—a folk-art church birdhouse converted into a lamp on one of her first buying trips to Los Angeles. The store owner was just transitioning it into a lamp when she walked in. She bought it on the spot. Turning it over she discovered Woodbury, Connecticut, carved into the bottom. A clue, perhaps, to its original home?

"We moved all our favorite things here," says Sharon. But coming from a huge house and shop in Wiscasset—three times the size of their new home and shop in Vinalhaven, they had to decide which favorites would make the cut. Always the architect, Paul advises, "Scale is the most important thing. Does it overpower a space, or does it blend in with the space?" We had to figure out which pieces would work and what to sell." Those pieces of painted-pine furniture that served them so well in Wiscasset came with them. "They served us and lives so beautifully," sighs Sharon, "and we were never tempted to sell them." She also makes it clear that Paul made certain that each piece had the perfect place. One piece that was never a question was the blue-painted cupboard that is now the centerpiece of their new kitchen (opposite). Sharon bought it in the early nineties from antique dealer Kathy Seibel, known as "the cupboard lady." "We went to her house," Sharon recalls, "found that cupboard, put it in our house and never offered it for sale. We moved it around a lot. In our library it stored games and films, and later a TV set in the bottom for the kids. Eventually, we moved it into the kitchen in Wiscasset, and now in our kitchen here. Hopefully, this is its final home," she laughs.

"All you need are cupboards and tables," says Sharon. That's what I always sold in my early shops, before Paul and I fell in love with French wares. The peg-top table (opposite) is almost the exact same blue as the cupboard behind it, has that same kind of family history. I've had it forever," claims Sharon. She bought it in Maine, part of an Ohio collection. In its former life in Wiscasset, it lived in their bedroom. It's all original, made in Pennsylvania, except the copper extensions that some clever person added to the legs to allow for more legroom when sitting or less bending over when preparing food—its current responsibility. When it's time for a break, for a sip of tea or glass of wine perhaps, a pair of stools pull up to it in yet another shade of blue (of course!). The collection of blue-and-white pitchers on the top shelf along the beadboard wall started with one," says Sharon. "But to be perfectly honest," she admits, "I have no idea which one that was." What she does know is that one led to another and another! "Whenever I would see one with a different stripe or coloration I'd have to have it."

"Everything we have kept and lived with," she reflects, "is tied to the practicality of our life, but falling in love came first. The things that we love are like old friends, and they are part of the family, a part of our home, and our kids have known them most of their lives."

Opposite: The kitchen nook is a study in shades of blue—the color Sharon and Paul associate with their life in Maine. The vintage blue cupboard and table have been part of their lives for many years, moving from room to room, storing everything from games and toys to a TV set. The collection of early New England baskets mixed with some old picnic baskets dangling from the ceiling are not just decorative but purposeful, used in different ways in the kitchen and, of course, on picnics.

Following pages: Hidden behind their shop on the first floor, facing out to the water, is Sharon and Paul's four-poster bed layered in romantic blues, with straw hats jauntily propped on each post. To the right of the green Shaker cupboard is Sharon's "greatest treasure"—a portrait with her mother by Anna B. McCoy, Jamie Wyeth's cousin.

"These are the things that make my heart soar."

Sharon Mrozinski

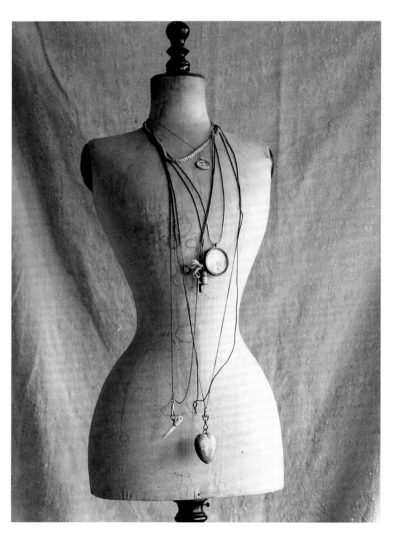

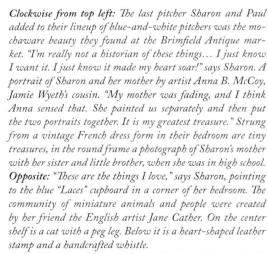

Clockwise from top left: The last pitcher Sharon and Paul added to their lineup of blue-and-white pitchers was the mochaware beauty they found at the Brimfield Antique market. *"I'm really not a historian of these things… I just know I want it. I just know it made my heart soar!"* says Sharon. A portrait of Sharon and her mother by artist Anna B. McCoy, Jamie Wyeth's cousin. *"My mother was fading, and I think Anna sensed that. She painted us separately and then put the two portraits together. It is my greatest treasure."* Strung from a vintage French dress form in their bedroom are tiny treasures, in the round frame a photograph of Sharon's mother with her sister and little brother, when she was in high school.

Opposite: *"These are the things I love,"* says Sharon, pointing to the blue "Laces" cupboard in a corner of her bedroom. The community of miniature animals and people were created by her friend the English artist Jane Cather. On the center shelf is a cat with a peg leg. Below it is a heart-shaped leather stamp and a handcrafted whistle.

Following pages: In the bedroom, Paul's architectural table is curated with Sharon's natural finds. As a child growing up in the middle of the desert she was left to roam and discover things. That passion for finding things—walking through the woods and picking up nests and abandoned turtle shells as never cooled. The taxidermy goose was a birthday present from Paul. She's never named him, but couldn't live without him. The little sculptural piece of bark in the basket reminds her of a ram's head.

Birds' nests were Sharon's first collection. She thinks because of her love of her home she is drawn to anything that gives shelter to any living body, whether it be a nest or a shell.

Opposite: The peaked cupboard in their bedroom is filled with Sharon's nest collection. She found most of them herself, like the mud swallow's nest from Brimfield and a few wasp nests, but some were gifts from Paul.

Clockwise from top right: Inside the cupboard on the lower shelf is a green box that is home to the nest and eggs of a wood thrush. An abandoned turtle's shell picked up on one of Sharon's frequent walks through the woods. In lieu of eggs, a pair of rocks are housed in a nest. "I am fascinated by what birds scavenge to build their nests," Sharon says. "Sometimes they are lined with horsehair or dandelions for softness. They are always looking for different things for their nest—just like us."

Inside the shop a great French blue cupboard stacked with early homespun linen sheets. The left door is held open with a carved cutting board and the right by a beautiful old mannequin decked out in a French apron in indigo.

A collection of bread-baking boards, originally thought to be Swedish, but later discovered to be from Turkey, squished together in an early wooden French farmhouse tub with metal-straps joinery. The lineup of porcelain soup bowls bloom bouquets of ebony-and-bone-handled knives with carbon-steel blades. On a line behind are strung coarse linen and cotton French workers' coats—the kind you might find Sharon wearing when she's hard at work at Marston House.

When asked if the aesthetic of their home on Vinalhaven is the same as their place in France, Paul answers, "It's the two of us. But I had to learn. In the beginning I didn't know anything about painted furniture," he confesses, "until Sharon brought me to New England for the first time in 1984. When we went to the Shaker Hancock Museum, and I was introduced to Shaker furniture, I thought I had gone to heaven." He fell in love with the craftsmanship, the proportions, the designs.

The evolution of that sensibility is seen in their bedroom and throughout the house—the closet doors, the latches. "But very important," Paul confirms, "this is Maine. You can't do this in France. It is for this site—It's site specific." Though the spirit of their lives in France is the same, the pieces are different, the execution is different. The color palette is different. In Provence, it's earth colors. It's sand. Here in Vinalhaven we are on the water. We wear blue. We live blue."

An armless unupholstered recliner with a foot stool from England. The bouquet was a gift from a neighbor's garden.

Paula Grief

LIVING
with
LESS

I first met Paula Grief in the late seventies. She had started her career at *Rolling Stone* under the famed art director Bea Feitler, and later after art directing for *Self* (where we met) and a few other magazine stints, she moved on to designing album covers, then working for the one and only Richard Avedon. By the eighties, she was directing and producing Super 8 rock videos. Not surprisingly, she married a rock musician client, and for twenty years they lived in a big house in Brooklyn where they raised their daughter. After they parted ways, and their daughter went off to school, they sold the house and Paula rented a little cottage in the Cobble Hill section of Brooklyn.

Though she had become a very successful director of TV commercials, one day inspired by the artful, yet functional pottery of Alexander Calder, Paula took a pottery class. Later when that passion for ceramics expanded, she read about an extraordinary Austrian potter named Lucie Rie. Rie had a studio in London mews and lived upstairs. Paula thought, "Wow, that's what I want to do." And so before long that inspiration led to her finding a ten-foot-wide, three-story storefront on the main street in Hudson, New York. She bought it in 2013 and in 2015, after a big renovation with help from her friend, the interior designer Steven Shadley, she moved in. She painted "PAULA" in gold on a black sign, matching the color of the house exterior and hung it over the front door.

Ten years later she is still there. Her storefront gallery and workshop are still on the ground floor, and though she continues to share her pottery in the big window facing Warren Street, she no longer welcomes strollers into the store. It's not that she's inhospitable, just practical. Over time she's discovered most serious collectors don't walk through the door but prefer to connect with her online and by appointment. Despite that decision she laughs, "I do get the funniest visitors banging on the window."

Off the studio there's a little porch where she can sit and gaze out at the rooftops beyond her backyard garden and the garage that is home to her treasured kiln and her space-saving car (a Fiat 500 Pop). Up the little staircase on the second floor, there's a cozy kitchen looking out to a balcony. Facing the street there's her sitting area with a long yellow sofa and a pair of, as she puts it, "funny chairs that turn into twin beds" when needed. The top floor is her personal nest and features a dresser, bench, bed and a surprisingly comfortable bathroom that fits a tub she loves to soak in at the end of the day.

Though her life here is quite spartan, Paula admits to having two storage units filled with things she just couldn't part with and certainly doesn't have space for. Her thought was that this would be her "city" house and she would eventually get a house in the country and that would be her "family" house. "This house," she admits, "is really just for me and I did it on purpose." Though she's not remorseful, there are moments like during the early years when her daughter Anna and friends would visit that she'd close the curtains on the ground floor store and set up her Walmart cots for them to sleep on. "It's almost like I went too far in downsizing," she muses. But what if she finds that "family" house to fill with all the things she has had on hold for the last ten years? Will she still need this sliver of a house on Warren Street? There is a bit of a pause as she reflects on an answer. "I'd never want to give up this place filled with so many things I can't live without and so many memories, but time will tell."

Previous page: Paula commissioned Earl Swanigan, a legendary artist in Hudson, to interpret a photograph of First Lady Jacqueline Kennedy by Richard Avedon, 1961. His efforts resulted in this huge canvas displayed on a dresser in her bedroom. The actual photograph is seen on the cover of the book in front of it, Jacqueline Kennedy: The White House Years.

Opposite: In her backyard, a porcelain work by Paula with three rounded levels. Because Paula is one of three sisters, she usually makes them in sets of three and calls them 'Sister' bottles.

Clockwise from top left: Paula's black store-front gallery and home on Warren Street since 2015, is ten feet wide and three stories high. She admits to being a "Bob Dylan completist." She has every record and book, including this tiny three-by-four-inch volume. The whimsical wooden box with her name on it was a gift from the mother of an old college boyfriend who found it at the Rose Bowl flea market in 1972. Paula at work on a new pot. She was inspired by the famed Austrian potter Lucie Rie.
Opposite: With most of her books in storage, and no place to put the ones she does have, Paula tucks those she can't live without through the rungs of her staircase.

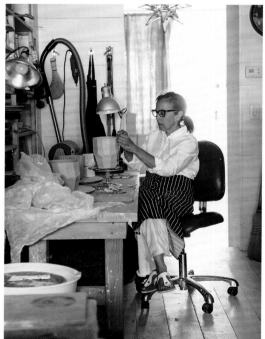

64

Above: Paula's spartan bedroom on the third floor is home to the dresser that displays her portrait of Jacqueline Kennedy, her bed, and a bench, one of a pair, that have lived with her in three different homes.
Right: Homage to Joan Didion's Play It As It Lays, *the 1970 first edition cover painted by Paula on an ashtray she made for a pottery exhibit in a Brooklyn bookstore almost ten years ago.*

Left: *Lined up against a large mirror in her cozy living room is one of Paula's "splotch" pitchers, a primitive wooden swan cutout she found at the Skoharie Antique Fair, a ceramic bird sculpture by artist Dan McCarthy, a tiny three-by-four-inch Bob Dylan volume next to a first edition volume of* Les Sculptures de Picasso. *Photographed by the Hungarian-French artist known as Brassaï in 1949, "It is always my inspiration," Paula says.*

Below: *If you don't know what a rain chain is, then take a look at the one Paula has hanging here. Normally, it would hang on the corner of a roof to guide the rain down like a spout. The drawing is by her daughter Anna, when she was in elementary school. The little face slotted into it and the portrait of Paula to the right were done by artist Dan McCarthy. Hanging between them is a black-clay hair pick created in Paula's studio by one of her former assistants and an artist in her own right. Sula Bermúdez-Silverman. Paula's "Tree of Life" stoneware platter floats below.*

Everything—walls, floors, ceilings, built-in-cabinets—are all paint-ed white. When asked how she keeps it so clean, she admitted, "It's not so clean. The floors are wrecked, but I sweep them every day, and I mop them once a week". For Paula, living with white opens everything up and against it every object has a way of standing out like this pair of Ethiopian carved wooden chairs she found at Craft Caravan, a legendary shop in SoHo almost forty years ago. "Sometimes," she says, "chairs are chosen not for comfort, but as art."

The way you display your objects either as a collection or as one- of-a-kinds—like Paula's trio of unrelated objects on a weathered Indonesian teak table on the porch, can connect them in a special way and tell their stories. From the left, an ashtray that reminds Paula of her mother—"not the body, but the hair and the face." A Paula vessel dangling a necklace of Eucaplytus berries, and a glazed flower made of leftover clay.

Clockwise from above: A stack of eclectic bowls. A pair of ceramic glazed birds by artist Dan McCarthy. A close-up up one of the Basquiat drawings seen on the wall. A collection of Paula's self-made home goods, a wooden eggcup from her ex-husband, and a silver pitcher that was a wedding present in 1983. The blue and beige ovals are by her friend and potter Michel Michael.

Opposite: Paula says she designed her kitchen around the bench, seen at left, one of a pair that has lived with her in three of her homes. Above it hangs a pair of drawings by her friend Jean-Michel Basquiat that he gave her in 1980. The Noguchi Pendant light over the wooden country table exemplifies her love of contrasts.

Joan Osofsky

LIVING
with
OLD & NEW

Joan Osofsky knows a thing or two about living with the things that you love. After moving five times, from a 1940's Dutch Colonial in suburban New Jersey—her first home in the seventies as a newlywed—to a Greek Revival house in Pine Plains, New York in the eighties with her husband, their daughter (13), and son (11), next door to what would become Hammertown Barn, the lifestyle store she opened in 1985. Next there was a short-lived stint (two years!) in 1999 to a colonial farmhouse surrounded by 65 acres of meadows and fields, a five minutes' drive from the Barn. And in 2011, after a divorce and children grown, she moved to a mid-1800s rental cottage nearby, and finally five years later to a charming 1929 cottage of her own in a small town in Connecticut. How did she decide what goes and what stays?

For starters there were the practical questions around space—would the big dining room table she loved fit? Or the oversize Swedish trunk? Or the old kitchen bookshelf with the original paint. If the answer was "no," then they along with other things were siphoned off to her kids or her friends or to the tent sales she holds annually in the front yard of the Hammertown house. But the real question was the one that matters most to her: What are the things that give my house soul?

Some of the things that fit into that category: her blue Le Creuset pot, part of a set that was a wedding present from her aunt; a reliable old French garlic press and George Jensen bread knife; her toleware tray collection started over 35 years ago, her tattered paperback of Julia Child's *The French Chef Cookbook*, the Windsor Chair bought in England at least three decades ago and held together here and there with pieces of string; her brass candlestick holders; her books; her primitive paintings; and, a sampler hand-stitched by her daughter. Each item, large or small, has the common ingredient of soulfulness that has given meaning, memory, and personality to all the places that have been her homes.

"Moving into a smaller house I wanted to have some order. I didn't want to feel claustrophobic with my stuff." says Joan. But on the other hand, she admits to still adding new things. "My house is all about old and new. There are the things I've carried with me that I could never part with—my keepers, but there are also new things that I have added like my collection of children's chairs that I started when my first my granddaughter was born." And though the old green trunk in front of her living room sofa fits into that former category, the pair of Swedish demilune tables were discovered recently to be a cozy dining room table. The brass candlestick on the mantelpiece have always been a favorite, but the framed calligraphy collection on the wall behind them was a new purchase by her daughter, who found the entire collection for sale at an outdoor antique show.

"As I get older," Joan muses, "and reflect on the joys and the challenges, I wouldn't change one thing in my life. All the bits and pieces make the memories." And that's what she tries to share with those who seek out things in her stores (there are three now), especially young people just starting their first homes. Her advice is to "Create your memories." To her that means choosing things made to last that tell a story. "Buy smart to have forever," she insists. That could be the bumper sticker on her heart—like the blue Le Creuset pot bubbling away on the stove or her ancient Windsor chair not fit to sit in anymore, but adding character nonetheless, and upstairs in her bedroom the folk art sampler her daughter Dana stitched for her thirty years ago. These are the things that make her happy, that tell her story every day. "Love where you live" has been her mantra from her first home when she was starting out as a young home maker to the cozy cottage she calls home now.

Previous page: It was over 35 years ago that Joan bought her first tole tray. Believing there is strength in numbers, she displays her favorite trays together. They hang over a 1800's hand-planed chest with sliding panels that she hunted down in Maine ages ago.

Opposite: To make one table Joan pushed together a pair of scalloped Swedish demilune tables. As much as she loves them, she admits they're not practical for family dinners. But, what can she do? She loves the table and loves the way the quartet of mid-century chairs look around them. "At my age," she says, " I'm not going to get rid of it.

"A home needs
things that give
it a soul."

Joan Osofsky

Above: After Joan stitched a sampler for her daughter, she returned the gesture with the sampler that hangs in Joan's bedroom. Our homes need those personal reminders of friendship.
Left: During one of her moves, Joan was cleaning out her kitchen, and asked herself, "Why do I need all these gadgets?" In the end she kept the French garlic press she's had for ever and the George Jensen bread knife that someone gave her. Just like her Le Cruset pot that she's had since she got married. Her advice—"Invest in quality and you'll have these things for the rest of your life."

Previous page: Joan's living room is a lively mix of old and new. The old wooden trunk ($25 at a tag sale) that she uses for a coffee table has been with her for a while, whereas the charming children's chairs in front of the fireplace are a new collection inspired by the birth of her first granddaughter. Joan has always collected the brass candesticks lining the mantelpiece, but the calligraphy collection of birds above is a new acquisition thanks to her daughter.

Right: Even before she had her first granddaughter Joan couldn't resist a child's chair. The high-back caned version on the left is Canadian, circa 1920. Its little sister, patented in 1872, is made of plywood with brass tacks spelling out (we assume) a mystery child's initials.

Below: Joan's passion is knitting. "It's such a good feeling to make something." Though this little sweater will probably go to her granddaughter Evie, she loves the idea that when she outgrows it, it might be framed and hung on her bedroom wall.

One of the biggest challenges when moving to a new home is not only what to let go of and then with that tough decision made—what to do with those things? When Joan met that challenge in one of her moves from big house to a smaller one she came up with a great idea: "I put everything on my porch that I didn't want and said to my son, 'Invite your friends up for the weekend. They can camp in the field and anything that's on this porch they can have. By the end of the weekend there was hardly anything left." What did remain (mainly pots and pans) she took to the local thrift shop.

And even though Joan carried a lot with her from home to home, she is always open to collecting new things. "A new house can sometimes require new and different things," she says. Like the collection of silhouettes grouped together over the bed in her guest room(opposite). She doesn't know how it happened. "I bought one or two and then I was hooked, and all of a sudden I had a collection." She also thinks they are very graphic and have a contemporary spirit.

People always ask Joan "How do you buy antiques?" And she always says to them that "you have to develop your eye. And that's how you'll make better choices." She shares a story about the time when she and her daughter, Dana, were in England and they met a friend who was studying for her masters in antiques at Christie's. Her professor told her, to "just go to the Portobello antique market and visit the best silver dealers. Go into places where you know you can't afford to buy anything. That's where you're really going to see quality things".

"Love what you love," Joan insists, "and don't follow senseless rules like—never mix periods. Rules become boundaries to developing your eye," she says. Case in point: Her purchase recently of an antique jelly cupboard with pierced-tin panels in the doors. When she saw it she recalled a home she had published in her last book. "It was an old barn filled with modern furniture and lighting, but in the living room there was this beautiful jelly cupboard with the pierced-tin panels. I never forgot it—the beauty of the contrasts." That's why she bought the jelly cupboard, even though it was very expensive. "I think it's just the patina of my age and doing what I'm doing for so long that I just trusted myself and I had to have it!" She put it in the store, and it sold the next day.

Joan's collection of silhouettes—one that seemed to develop serendipitously—grouped on a wall in her guest bedroom have a contemporary spirit. Her favorite is the one of Dana's two daughters—her granddaughters, at the far right.

Joan bought her Windsor chair in England over thirty years ago. Legend has it that King George III discovered what he called a "stick" chair in the town of Windsor and was so impressed with its comfort that he had them made for the palace. No matter the provenance, Joan believes antique and heirloom pieces—a chair, a table, a cupboard, or a rug—add character and integrity to our homes.

Let sleeping dogs lie (wherever they want!) It's not just things that that make our homes happy. Don't forget about our pets. There's nothing as comforting as a dog sleeping cozily in front of an open fire or resting on a pile of vintage Kantha quilts like Etta, Joan's little sidekick, who just passed away after fifteen years by her side.

Clockwise from top left: Step through the front door of Joan's house and you're face-to-face with the stairs covered in a graphic woven-wool runner. Joan and Etta. At the foot of the stairs is a 1930 hooked rug from Maine. The late nineteenth-century green umbrella stand just inside the door is a treasured find from France.
Opposite: *Climb up the stairs and you can peek into Joan's cozy guest room under the roofline, where she's added a skylight to bring in more sun during the days and view the stars at night. Her neatly organized shelves display favorite books, coverlets, sewing and knitting projects, and groupings of family photos.*

Along the mantelpiece a chorus line of brass candlesticks that Joan's been collecting for years. "They call to me the way the tole trays do." Interspersed are special little treasures like the boot strap knife holder(far right), bought in France from her good friends Sharon and Paul Mrozinski (see their story on page 34), a petite shoe found in a baroque antique shop in a barn in Lincolnville, Maine, and in the center, a painted tole box, the resting place of her beloved golden retriever Abby's ashes.

Mary Emmerling

LIVING with RED, WHITE & BLUE

Everyone that loves what we think of as "country" style knows Mary Emmerling. Her books, starting with *American Country* in 1980, are legendary, but, when we first met, she was Mary Ellisor and I was Mary Carter—two single girls living in New York City and working at *Mademoiselle* Magazine. Looking back on those days, she loves to remind me "that we were there at the best of times. It was a blast!" she exclaims. In many ways those days were also a blast-off for her, as she started to share her home style in those pages as the first Home Furnishing Editor of the magazine.

Over time Mary started her own magazine, opened a fabled country store in East Hampton and one in New York City, published thirty-six books, and let's not forget—raised a daughter and son (now both grown) and is now a grandmother to Bixie, age eight. And then there are the homes (almost as many as her books!) that she's created in New York City, the Hamptons, Key West, Des Moines, Phoenix, Santa Fe, and now a cozy shingled cottage in the Hamptons (right down the block from the one she lived in the late seventies.)

When you push open the gate of the white picket fence (what else?) with an American flag flapping from a pole nearby to greet you (there are three more in the backyard) and start to knock on her front door, there's no need for she has seen you coming, and before you know it there's the hug and you're welcomed into the warmth of Mary Emmerling's world.

All the things she has always loved and carried with her to make each house her home are right in front of you. Starting with the long wooden peg rack just inside filled with all the hats she wears—four kinds of cowboy hats, a Yankees baseball cap, one decorated with an American flag and another that says, 'Best Day Ever.' Dangling in between are faded jean jackets, a fringed western jacket, a colorful striped serape, an American flag poncho, and a patched indigo backpack with a faded flag scarf flowing out of it.

Originally a waystation for potatoes, Mary bought the house almost three years ago "sight unseen." She had been living in Santa Fe, and before that twenty-one years in Phoenix, but the thought that kept haunting her was, "Should I move back to New York to be with my kids and my granddaughter?" When she hinted to her family that she was thinking of coming back, her son-in-law, Nicholas, jumped on his computer and found it. Turns out it was a little shingled cottage just a block away from where they had once lived. When she sent a friend to check it out, she called and said excitedly, "Mary, it has your name written all over it." And then she knew the answer to her question—"Yes, it's time for me to move back and make a home again for me, my children and my granddaughter, Bixie."

So, she packed up all the things she couldn't live without—the blue-and-white spongeware, her signature turquoise jewelry, the black-and-white photography she has carefully collected, the books that celebrate the art and places she has loved, the one-of-a-kind paintings, the Native American pottery and textiles, the white ironstone and little silver dishes, the stars and stripes on flags, denim jackets and artifacts, her well-worn and loved cowgirl boots, her jeweled high-top sneakers, her walking sticks, skulls, and hundreds of hearts and crosses—and carefully found a place for them. You might think this world of disparate objects might collide and clutter the whitewashed rooms of her cozy two-story cottage, but instead Mary has found ways to give each collection and memento the space it deserves so that the stories, the persons, the places they represent all come together to create the soul and personal spirit of her home.

Previous page: Mary loves peg racks. The long one just inside her front door is filled with some of her favorite hats, sweaters, jackets, and bags.
Opposite: Mary has a thing for blue and white. Her collection of spongeware, like the pitchers and bowls opposite is a testament to that. She began picking pieces up on her travels as a young decorating editor for Mademoiselle. *"I couldn't spend much then," she admits, "so most of them had cracks that I had to find ways to hide when I displayed them.*

Once Mary had found the perfect cottage to create a summer home to share with her daughter, Samantha, her son-in-law Nicholas, her son Jonathan, and his daughter, Bixie—the deliveries began nonstop. Some were things chosen from her apartment in Santa Fe and others were a bounty of new things hunted down in her favorite antique shops in Round Top, Texas. At one point, her very good (and very patient!) friend who was overseeing all these comings-and-comings, sent up a red alert: "Mary, all these things are never going to fit! I think you've gone crazy!" Mary calmly explained that she knew exactly how everything would fit. After all, her whole career had been about setting up photo shoots, creating showrooms—making things fit. And as predicted everything did, except, she admits, one little table, that she put outside on the street as a giveaway. And it was gone in five minutes.

Previous page: Without a doubt the woman who lives here has been touched by the spirit of Georgia O'Keeffe. There's the bleached white skull of a mighty elk gazing down upon the black and white image of a church in Taos, photographed by our friend Buffy Birrittella, the coffee table—an old wooden door, and in contrast a romantic English turn-of-the century gilded chandelier.

Top left: Mary discovered the work of constructivist artist Ryan Carey in California in the early eighties and featured his artful vessels in her 1984 book American Country West. *When she moved into her new house, Chris Mead, an old friend and longtime book collaborator gave her a call. "I have a present for the new house," he said. "Come and get it." That meant a quick ride to English Country Home, his iconic store in Bridgehampton, where he reached up on a high shelf and presented her with one of the Ryan Carey's pots he had collected with her many years ago on another book shoot. Now, it sits in a special spot in her new home, one of her favorite pieces of art collected from all those book-making travels.*

Left: When Mary's big flag is flying from the picket fence in front of the house it means "I'm home. You're welcome!"

Opposite: If you want to take a walk at Mary's, just grab a cane from her one-of-a-kind collection poking out of a pair of glazed pots lined up in the front hallway. While you're at it, you could grab one of her American flags gathered like a bouquet of red, white, and blue. On the Fourth of July and other patriotic holidays, you'll see them flying from the pickets of her fence.

"I love everything out in the open."

Mary Emmerling

Clockwise from top left: An iconic zebra-striped copy of the romantic I Married Adventure *by Osa Johnson, is a backdrop for a bracelet of charms. Related to two American presidents—William Henry Harrison (9th) and his grandson Benjamin Harrison (23rd), Mary grew up in a house full of flags. She is always on the lookout for more to add to her display during patriotic holidays; the miniature silver sombrero made in Mexico is part of what Mary calls a "fun" collection. She has an artist make little stands for them.*

Opposite: Being a writer of books herself, it's not surprising that Mary is passionate about her book collection and is always finding interesting ways to display them in her new home. Here a stack of coffee table books become a pedestal for a bold pot of flowers.

What would be the perfect centerpiece of Mary's cottage kitchen? Certainly not a modern marble-top island (no sirree!). For Mary it would be a perfectly imperfect greenish-blue-painted table with a handy shelf underneath to store stacks of blue-and-white ironstone compotes filled with mini candy bars, yellowware bowls of potatoes. On top, there is plenty of room for English cutting boards, a giant blue-and-white graniteware bowl, and a Coca-Cola bucket filled with blooming zinnias. "The table always has too much on it," she laughs, "but I use it all, and I like it in plain sight.

When it's time for supper, there's plenty of room for the whole family and a couple of friends to pull up a chair to this old, weathered farm table and enjoy burgers scooped off the grill, corn on the cob, and big slices of juicy heirloom tomatoes—all local fare picked up from the farmstand down the road. Or when it's one of those really hot summer nights, the legs of the table are folded up and it's carried to the backyard where dinner is served alfresco. The table, along with the set of chairs with the woven-leather backs, were Round Top finds.

Clockwise from top left: Mary loves everything out in the open, like her Concho-patterned silverware stored in a cozy basket. Two still lifes in the kitchen—a freshly made lemon poppy seed bundt cake compliments of her friend Reg already sampled, and another still life featuring The New York Times *done in crayon by artist Don Gray. She bought the painted Coca-Cola bucket for her son, Jonathan. Sometimes she fills it with ice and bottles of Coke (his favorite), and sometimes she fills it with fresh flowers like these zinnias from the local farmstand. "When I worked at* House Beautiful *we would joke and call it* House *"Bluetiful," as any house that we shot that had blue in it would end up on the cover,"* Mary jokes. She started to collect anything blue, but especially faded blue cupboards like the one opposite. "Blue and white keeps everything clean and fresh looking," she shares. "And, in a beach cottage, it's the blue of the ocean and the white of the sand." The fish artwork above it is from Mary's collection by artist Don Gray.

When Mary was working on her first book, *American Country*, she traveled out West to explore that special kind of country living. When she hit Santa Fe in 1978, she discovered the turquoise jewelry that has become one of her most-prized possessions, and her most personal accessory. "In those days the pawn shops were filled with it," she recalls, "and so I could afford to pick up the most beautifully crafted bracelets and necklaces and special pieces." When she came back East, they became her trademark, along with cowboy boots, bandannas, and all manner of cowboy chapeaus. There was something about that home-on-the-range style that seemed to fit, and so it wasn't long before it became part of the way she dressed and the way she lived.

An altar to turquoise and silver, Mary's bedroom dresser is curated with a silver tray serving up some her favorite bracelets against an impromptu exhibition of favorite photographs in a collection of silver frames from Mexico and South America. Dangling from a cross are layers of her silver-and-turquoise necklaces another of Mary's passions. On the wall behind, where you might expect to see a mirror, Mary has hung a painting by artist Don Gray. When he was painting Bloomingdale's displays from his apartment window right across Lexington Avenue, Mary had a store right up the street. As fate would have it, after both were living in Phoenix, Mary got a call from a friend that Don had passed away and left a house full of his art. When Mary went there and asked about his early art created during those Bloomingdale's days, it was suggested she would not like them because they were "kind of primitive." Mary saw them and said, "I'll take them all."

Susan Zises

LIVING
with
AN ARTISTIC
SPIRIT

When Susan Zises walked into the front door of what had been the carriage house of a stately summer home in the Hamptons and saw the wrought iron circular staircase and the old wooden floors beneath it, her mind was made up in an instant—"I'll take it!" she said. In an attempt to downsize she had recently sold a much larger farmhouse nearby and was in search of a cozier getaway from her home base in Manhattan. That was twenty years ago, and since then, other than the staircase and the old floors everything else she has kind of invented.

Susan is an artist and interior designer, so this invention is not surprising. She added a large sunny studio with room upstairs for her three adult children, (she and their father divorced many years ago, but are still good friends), their spouses, and her seven grandchildren to visit. And when she decided it would be nice for all of them to celebrate Thanksgiving in the main house, she added a glass room. "It was a kit and easier said than done," she admits. And that was after securing all the permits and the things she had to do before construction could even begin. But "well worth it," she sighs, "as I'm out here pretty much all the of the year and live in that room."

"I don't believe in comfort at all," says Susan with a laugh. Take the large antique French sofa(opposite), stripped of its needlepoint upholstery except for a lone piece remaining on the outside of one of the arms. When she moved it in, she decided it was way too much color for her, so she tried to dim it with black magic markers. When that didn't work she "ripped it all off." "There's horsehair under the burlap covering on the back and who knows what else. No one sits there," she confesses, "but I can't get rid of it—I love it." And then there are the two wooden chairs in her sunny living room. One is a French prototype, and the other is from the Orkney Islands. Both look more like artful sculptures than places to rest, but thankfully for her family and guests she has provided a couple of comfortable sofas and well-cushioned chairs all covered in serviceable white canvas. Oh, and lest we forget, there's room for more on her black leather Barcelona daybed that's near her shiny black grand piano and a romantic white ceramic Swedish stove. (It's evidence of her love for the style of the Gustavian period). The stove is just for show; as an electrician advised her it was likely a fire hazard if put to use. She stuck an electric heater inside, but never turns it on as the house is drafty, but warm. Greeting all that enter is another Swedish collectible—a crystal chandelier with two rows of candle lights suspended to the right of the stairway, which took her breath away on that first visit. "Though it cost a fortune I have no idea if it's worth anything. It was a prop used for tent parties." She and one of her daughters wired it—"but never properly," she guesses. Some of the light bulbs are burned out and some are missing, but she likes it like that. "It would be wrong if it they were all lit. It would be too perfect."

When she lived in a larger house and apartment, Susan allowed herself to find a place for everything she loved. "I had four daybeds in the living room of my old apartment. It didn't occur to me that that was a problem because I loved daybeds. It didn't feel cluttered to me. It felt fine. Here, my sensibility has become a lot less cluttered—pretty spare," she says. "But everything has a story. Everything I love is sort of forever."

Previous page: A Swedish chandelier of crystals and candlelight is not the welcome you would expect upon entering what was once a simple carriage house. The quartet of Chinese glazed pots displayed on the table below it became an instant collection. Pinned on the wall above is one of four pastel drawings of Greek busts, probably an art student's project.
Opposite: A French countess was responsible for needlepointing the entire sofa. Susan removed most of the ragged needlepoint, leaving a few remnants as evidence of the countess's work.

No, this is not a set from an Ingmar Bergman film, but certainly the director would have approved its spirit of romance and intrigue. Susan's baby grand piano makes for a perfect prop. (Does she play? "Yes, poorly!") Adding to the mood is the Swedish ceramic stove (that's never been lit to avoid the threat of fire). The chandelier once used as an actual prop, sets the mood impeccably as does the skeletal wooden chair with its back to the piano. But hold on, what's that sleek Mies van der Rohe Barcelona couch doing there? Susan fell in love with pro-modernist design in the sixties when she was a student at Pratt Institute. When she got married she had to have the couch for her first apartment, along with Arco lamps, and seven Saarinen tables. Would Ingmar approve? She likes to think that, in-between takes, he might have enjoyed stretching out on it for a quick nap or *(kort tupplur!)*

The beautiful original wood floors were one of the features that instantly sold Susan on this old carriage house. She would never cover them with a rug or carpet. She loves their bareness and the warm tones of the boards, their irregularity, the nailheads, and how they how they fit together like a wooden patchwork. The white boarded walls are bare, too, except for a black-and-white abstract by Vermont artist Michael Singer and a vintage French gilded mirror.

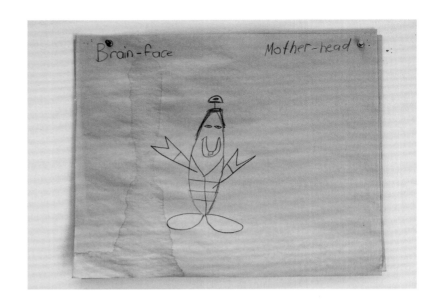

"Everything I love is sort of forever."

Susan Zises

Clockwise from top left: "I love that you can barely see yourself in the cloudy glass of this French gilded mirror," laughs Susan. "You always look fabulous when you look at yourself." A yellowed pencil sketch by her son Oliver is push-pinned into the wall of an upstairs bedroom. "I have no idea what it means," she says, "but it's a memory of that little boy of long ago." A chair that was once made by locals on the remote Orkney Islands stands in Susan's sunroom. Decorated with a giant necklace of wooden beads it looks a bit like a timeless throne.

Opposite: Though her creamy white Swedish stove does nothing to stave off the occasional chill of a damp day by the sea, Susan could never give it up for something more practical. She's always had a thing for Swedish stoves and had one in her previous home. At the time she didn't realize that it was against code, and so her new stove stands like a beautiful sculpture whose brass door will never open to reveal a cozy fire.

The wrought iron staircase that stole Susan's heart the first moment she saw it is stamped with the name of the London iron fabricator that made it. While watching an old English movie, Susan spied a similar staircases making its way out of the Underground. That's when she decided that's where her staircase first lived. If you traipse up the stairs you will find a lantern at the top, which if her theory holds, lit the way for tube riders on a foggy London night.

Susan calls this her "baby" staircase. It's an American handcrafted 3D model that architects would show to their clients so they could understand dimensional perspectives. Over the years they have become a popular collectible. The roundness of this and her wrought iron staircase was Susan's inspiration for the round shape of the doors entering her Garden Room, seen through the real staircase opposite

Left: Look under the piano on pages 108 and 109 and you'll spot Susan's hidden treasure of four ancient Greek urns. Did she discover them on an archaeological adventure? No, not exactly!. She recollects (though long ago) buying one from an antique shop in Greenwich Village and then she had to have more. They lived with her in her apartment in New York, then in her former larger farmhouse, and once she moved to these smaller digs she stuck them under the piano! "Why not?" she asks. "They would have looked silly on top of the piano." And that's that.

Following pages: The first addition to the carriage house was the Garden Room. It was meant to be a porch made of doors strung together. The windows were supposed to pop out and screens to go in, but once the frames were painted the windows were permanently sealed. "So, instead," Susan laughs, "it became a not-a-screen-porch." In this room each chair is a character particularly the two on either side of the wooden carved mask. The one on the left accessorized with giant wooden beads is from the Orkney Islands. The one on the right is a French prototype. "It's very uncomfortable," Susan states, "but I don't believe in comfort at all."

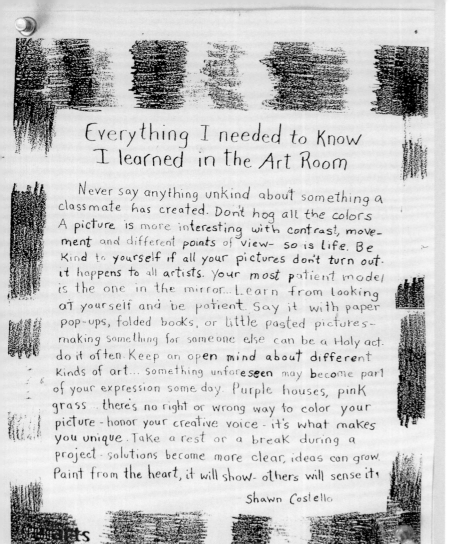

Everything I needed to Know
I learned in the Art Room

Never say anything unkind about something a classmate has created. Don't hog all the colors A picture is more interesting with contrast, movement and different points of view- so is life. Be Kind to yourself if all your pictures don't turn out. it happens to all artists. Your most patient model is the one in the mirror...Learn from looking at yourself and be patient. Say it with paper pop-ups, folded books, or little pasted pictures-making something for someone else can be a Holy act. do it often. Keep an open mind about different Kinds of art... something unforeseen may become part of your expression some day. Purple houses, pink grass ...there's no right or wrong way to color your picture - honor your creative voice - it's what makes you unique. Take a rest or a break during a project - solutions become more clear, ideas can grow. Paint from the heart, it will show- others will sense it,

Shawn Costello

Clockwise from top left: A note Susan found hanging at Pearl Paint, an iconic art supply store in New York City. A needlepoint message she takes to heart. The back entrance of the studio with a wisteria vine that according to Susan is devouring the house. The artist can usually be found in her studio. Here she is with some of her latest works on paper.
Opposite: Susan's trompe l'oeil garden orb made out of roof sheeting and rivets beneath a subject she's obsessed with—chandeliers. (The shears are real.)
Following pages: An impromptu exhibit on the wall of Susan's studio. The giant rhododendron (84" x 54") oil on canvas is from her botanical series. The black evening gowns, oil and collage on paper, are a tribute to Dior.

Willie & Mari Binnie

LIVING with STORIES

Behind this big red door lies the special world of William and Mari Binnie. Both teachers at Williams College right up the road (she art history; he oil painting and drawing), they used to pass this house many times. "But then," they recall, "it was a peeling, drab kind of green with brown doors." One day driving by in 2018, they saw a woman putting a For Sale by Owner sign in the yard. Having tired of living in faculty housing for almost nine years, they decided to take a look. After a three-and-a-half-hour visit with the eighty-year-old owner, they wrote her a letter and bought the house later that year. They moved in with Scout, their sweet scruffy dog, and eventually welcomed two daughters,—Paloma and Pia.

"It was really in poor shape on the outside," Willie began, "and pretty dim on the inside, made darker by all the quilts the owner had covered the windows with." An open staircase running from the living room on the main floor up to the third level, where cozy bedrooms are tucked into the tip top of the house, made it feel more like an indoor tree house. And adding to that Swiss Family Robinson feeling were old hand-hewn timber beams throughout. According to Willie they were rescued in the early seventies by a local man who had been hired by the owners of the property to burn down an old barn up the hill. When he saw the old timbers, the barn's fate took a different turn. "You can't burn this barn down," he told the owners with great conviction, "it's the oldest timber in Hancock." So instead of burning it down, the owners offered it to him and sold him a parcel of land. Out of all the hand-hewn pieces of chestnut and oak he salvaged from the old barn, he built a lodge on the existing eighteenth-century foundation. The first person to live in it was a retired New York firefighter who retooled a little of the interior—notably sinking the living room and adding the massive stone fireplace, giving it, as Willie puts it "a bit of a 1970s ski lodge vibe." And then, if you believe in destiny, the firefighter artistically embedded among the fireplace stones a fragment of a Roman frieze rescued from a museum dumpster filled with decommissioned plaster molds of antiquities no longer needed for teaching. When Willie and Mari saw it there, it was as if it was left as a welcome sign to their artistic sensibilities.

Willie grew up on a ranch in East Texas. Mari grew up in Puerto Rico. They met in the autumn of 2013 when Willie was working on his masters at SMU and Mari was a visiting professor working on her PhD at University of Texas in Austin. The big leap of faith came when she left for a year in Brazil on a Fulbright Fellowship, and he joined her in São Paulo. They tied the knot legally in 2015 in Dallas with beer and barbeque but had their actual wedding ceremony in January 2016 at a nineteenth-century lighthouse on a small island eight miles off the mainland of Puerto Rico. To mark that day they buried mementos in the sand. On visits back they've tried to find them, but the hurricanes swept them away long ago. Walking through their home it is easy to see that those lost mementos have been replaced by other things they've collected along the way that fill their home with memories and meaning.

"Things find you," Willie reflects, "and accumulate and nearly every single little thing in the house has some sort of origin story—some very meaningful and personal, others as simple as finding it on the street somewhere and deciding it needed a home. In the end," says Willie, "it all conspires to create a space that feels very warm and tells stories without being too precious or claustrophobic." They both agree for them the most important thing is making their home comfortable. During the winter they spend most of their time sitting in front of the fire. "We call it Hippie TV," laughs Willie.

Page 123: After a nighttime witch tour in Salem, Massachusetts, where they spied some of the historic houses painted in deep-umber tones, Mari and Willie decided to paint theirs jet-black, and the front door red.

Previous pages: When they saw the broken plaster cast—a fragment of a Roman frieze(opposite)—embedded within the stones of the massive fireplace, they felt it was a sign that this was just the place for an art historian and an artist to create a home for themselves, and now two daughters.

Clockwise from top left: Willie's guitar nook displays the last of his music gear from playing in bands throughout his teens and twenties. The patches sewn on Willie's backpack are souvenirs of their travels. Willie has a store of tributes to his father's Scottish heritage, including his grandfather's WWI medals. The novelty tourist pens are a tradition the whole family enjoys. They have over 250.

Opposite: The enormous encyclopedia belonged to Willie's father's. Willie adored it as child and still does. "It has wonderful illustrations and is a beautiful object itself." The map of South America above it is thought to be from the forties or early fifties because, as Willie discovered, "Brasilia, the capital of Brazil, is not yet on the map." It was a lighthearted gift to Mari whose research mostly involves Brazil and the greater region.

The centerpiece of the dining room table is a collection of "drippy" bees-wax candles. Above them hangs a brutalist pendant lamp—a sixties copper-and-glass piece Willie found in Milan. He thinks what un-consciously attracted him to it were the orange glass forms that to him were very reminiscent of the sacred Sankara Stones in Indiana Jones the Temple of Doom. *The gallery behind the bar consist mainly of art by friends. The portrait of Scout(right wall) was painted by Wil-lie when he was teaching a portraiture class. He framed it in gold as Scout seemed so "regal."*

131

The carved-wood beaver with brush and palette in paw is actually the mascot of the Binnie home. He came to live there, in another life-time, when Willie's studio was the Beaverpond Gallery. The former owner felt it only right that he should remain, and rather than get rid of him or hide him away, he lives rather happily in a garret guest room above Willie's studio.

Willie's grandfather died in Scotland before he was born, but his memory is very much alive in their home thanks to all the Scottish ephemera not only given to him by his father but collected in used bookstores and antique shops over the years. This traditional Scottish bagpiper counts the seconds with an hourglass displayed on a stack of tattered Scottish works by the likes of Sir Walter Scott and Robert Burns.

Clockwise from top left: Mari and Willie take a breather in their sunlit living room. A little ceramic pumpkin made by Willie in second grade is now an incense holder. The matchbooks were designed by the couple for their wedding in Puerto Rico in 2016. They had to order a case and didn't realize that it was 2,500 match-books. (They are set for life!) With a collection of WPA national parks posters, (below and op-posite), a striped woolen Pendleton blanket on the bed, and vintage skis overhead, the guest apartment Mari and Willie created over the garage studio allows visitors to feel as if they were camping out in a snug cabin in the forest. A silver goblet celebrating the birth of their first daughter, Paloma.

Following pages: While the garage space was a studio in the eighties, it is now Willie's draw-ing wall.

Bethann Hardison

LIVING
with
A LIGHTER
LOAD

Bethann Hardison has made the apartment on these pages in New York City her home for fifty years. I think it was almost that long ago that I met her. I was the Beauty Editor of *Mademoiselle* magazine and she was working for the iconic designers Stephen Burrows and Willi Smith. I had invited her to speak at a little informal symposium about the meaning of beauty. How ironic that all these years later she has co-directed and starred in *Invisible Beauty*, a documentary about her legendary life and groundbreaking advocacy for Black models.

Over the decades Bethann and I have stayed in touch. I knew her mantra was "The lighter the load, the freer the journey," so when I reached out to her in the summer of 2020 and asked if she would share her story about living with the things you love, she laughed and accused me of being "a defensively borderline hoarder." I countered with, "Well, I'm not a hoarder exactly…" And before I could finish, she volleyed back with "That's what every good collector says." And she was right. But as I survey the paintings on her walls, the piles of neatly stacked books, the curation of sculptures and knick-knacks lining her tabletops, mantel and shelves, the nests of baskets, her dresser decorated with jewelry and spiritual totems, it's hard to say this is a woman who follows her own advice and is totally committed to living without!

"How could I give up everything?" she asks, looking around at the walls in her living room. There's the artwork of Jean-Michel Basquiat, Keith Haring, David Bowie, and Andy Warhol for starters—all were personal friends. There's a collection of colorful Haitian paintings connected to the memory of a friend she was in business with years back. Everything has a story that in its own way tell hers, and giving them up would be leaving what she refers to as her "Home Home" without memory and color. These are things, she says, that "delight your environment." And

though she could never give them up she believes there are ways to lighten your environment without ditching everything.

She sees her apartment as her base with two distinct feelings. The living room, which is very open is like a loft flooded with daylight. The artwork is bold and colorful. There are no curtains on the windows, and the parquet floors are bare, except in the winter when she layers them with her treasured collection of Moroccan rugs. Entering her bedroom is like walking into another world. The color of the living room, apart from her dresser top, an altar of colorful beads and jewelry watched over by a pair of statues of Yemanya, the Brazilian goddess of the sea gives way to a sea of white. Here, the artwork is represented by black-and-white photographs. Although Bethann never considered herself a "real" model, it was she and group of Black models that brought the world of French fashion to their feet as they strode across the stage at the historic Battle of Versailles fashion show in 1973. She also was at the helm of her own eponymous model and management agency, which became a legendary advocate for Black models in the world of fashion.

"I like space. I need air," she declares. "Clutter is so dangerous. I love NO things. It's very difficult to release things. You really have to struggle with it." And then she commands softly—"Let it go…let it go!"

Previous page: On the top of Bethann's bedroom dresser overseeing her collection of jewelry and personal totems is a phalanx of spiritual icons led by the Brazilian goddess of the sea, Yemanya. *Opposite:* In a corner of the living room a solid wooden cupboard is flanked by a pair of sensuous carved sculptures.balanced on top of stereo speakers. The figure on the right holding aloft a map of Africa was an unexpected birthday gift. The blue sign once displayed in an African barber shop suggests six dapper styles the client might choose from.

Bethann's living room gallery of art displays mostly gifts from friends, including on the far right over the lilies a Keith Haring collage and above that an early Jean-Michel Basquiat. She's never been to Haiti but loves all the Haitian art that a friend, who knew all the artists personally, passed on to her. The table and benches are where you'll likely find her toiling away at her next project—a much-anticipated memoir.

Buddha's hand gestures are called mudras and each has a specific meaning. The one depicted in these graceful metal hands symbolizes the continuous energy of the cosmic order as coming from the heart. It's not surprising, that they sit prominently on Bethann's worktable, seen on the previous page.

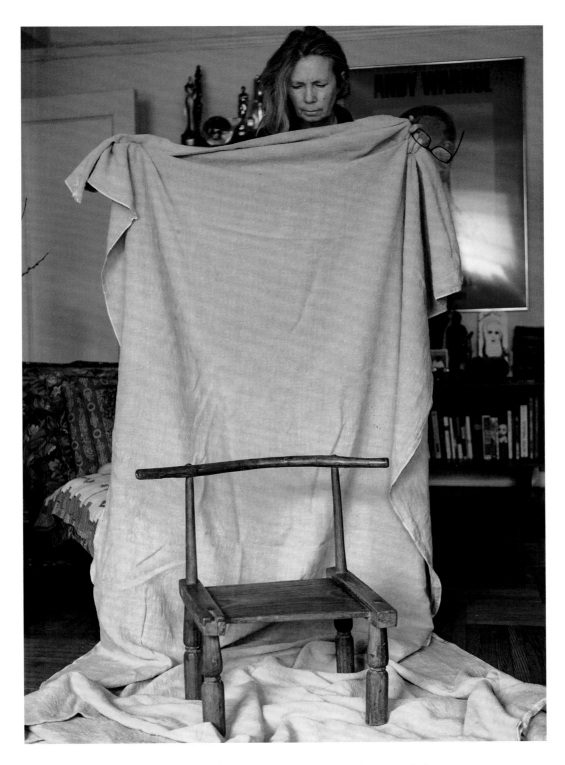

Yes, that's me looking down on one of Bethann's loved objects—a little
African wooden chair, more like a piece of sculpture, that was a wedding present. "All of my wedding presents were from Craft Caravan," admits Bethan. "It was one of those unique emporiums one
would find wandering the cobbled streets of SoHo in its early days."
Its devoted owners—Ford Wheeler and Ignacio Villarreaz and his
wife, curated it like an inspiring gallery that specialized in African
design objects and art. Sadly, it's closed.

"I love no things, but sometimes you get things and they're wonderful and they have a purpose"

Bethann Hardison

Clockwise from top left: Staring out from the top of Bethann's bedroom dresser is a Mexican Day of the Dead skull. (See it surrounded by other symbolic icons on page 139). Gucci brand creative director Allesandro Michele gifted Bethann this monagrammed throw. He told her he purposely created it that way "because it reminded him of this grandmother's stuff." One night at Mr. Chow's in New York City, Bethann had dinner with the artist Keith Haring and "he took a bowl and drew on it," she says. Later she decided to clean it a bit, and was horrified when the artwork started to disappear! "I had no idea the ink would erase!" she exclaims.

Opposite: "I'm a basket person," Bethann proclaims. "I never carry a real purse, always an ethnic straw bag." A few pieces from Bethann's collection of woven baskets from different regions of Africa, including a carved wooden mask laying on its side.

A fireplace that actually works, a chaise comfortably layered with a Moroccan throw, a sheepskin, and stacks of pillows, and the wonderful centerpiece of it all—Bethann's big boy bike! —all add character and warmth to her living room. "I love my bicycle," she exclaims. "I always had a boy's bike. I never wanted a girl's bike. I was a tomboy at heart." "Because it's so heavy (a cruiser) no one's ever tried to steal it," she laughs. The library case(at right), picked up from a second hand shop many years ago, stores glassware and silver—all wedding presents. On top is a collection of unique statues, including a fertility doll, mostly from South Africa.

On the mantelpiece leans a mirror with an optimistic message for every day of the year surrounded by a mix of meaningful objects, including a Buddha candle and an ostrich egg from Cape Town. When Bethann spotted the curlicue-gilded frame in a thrift store, she recognized the person of the placeholder picture as a famous model she had known during her modeling days. "Guests are always curious about who she is, but I've never replaced her," says Bethann.

Clockwise from left: In the peacefulness of Bethann's bedroom, all the bold and eclectic color of the living room is replaced by spartan white bedding (not a wrinkle in sight) and transparent window sheers that give off a kind of ghostly glow. Her energy is captured in the portrait over the bed by photographer Steven Meisel in the 80s is in contrast to the quiet reflectiveness of her mood above. On the wall over a South African carved wooden chair is a meaningful trio of images of her mother, herself, and her young granddaughter. Bethann's son is Kadeem Hardison, an actor who first came to prominence in his role as Dwayne Wayne on A Different World. "He is," she says, "the nicest human on this earth." A tablet of the Koran, that she brought back from one of her yearly visits to Morocco.

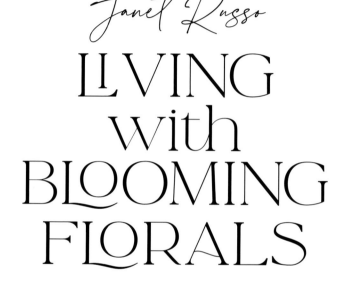

Janet Russo

LIVING
with
BLOOMING
FLORALS

It was the photograph of romantic floral sundresses (ten or so) gently floating from an old rope clothesline in a sunny backyard in Nantucket that set my heart atwitter more than twenty years ago. It sealed my love for the style, and vintage fabrics, that became the design signature (and heart) of Janet Russo and her eponymous brand.

Janet was well on her way with a charming, shingled boutique on the main street of Nantucket when William Waldron a young photographer, was tasked with capturing a bit of her world for *House & Garden* magazine in 1989. I don't know what part of her world struck me first—the clothesline photograph or when I walked into her magical shop. The point is all these years later—after moves from Nantucket to Kent, Connecticut, to New York City, to Newport, Rhode Island (right after 9/11), and now to nearby Bristol with her husband, Bill Jacklin, and their daughter, Jasmine—that Janet Russo style is still in full bloom.

And when I say in full bloom I mean blooming from all parts of her world—from the floral dresses she still designs to the stacks of vintage floral fabrics she still collects to the curtains, cushions, spreads, tablecloths, and even wallpaper she still decorates every inch of their home with. And let's not forget the giant bouquets of flowers (real and artificial) blooming out of vintage pots and vases on the kitchen counter, on the dining room table, and in smaller doses next to beds and on bathroom sinks. Janet Russo has always lived in nostalgic, magical garden-like environments. Way back when her cozy cottage in Nantucket couldn't contain it all, she transplanted the romantic blooms of her personal designs and the charming spirit of her home into her own boutiques. She opened the first one in Nantucket with a friend, but it wasn't long before she took over sole ownership. When she opened the door to her first New York City shop on Madison Avenue and 91st Street in the eighties, it was her handwritten name on the sign above it that welcomed everyone in.

In 1990 she confirms, she met Bill Jacklin, a dashing Englishman and internationally renowned artist, on a blind date set up by mutual friends. His work then was centered on capturing iconic New York City life in places like Central Park, the Meatpacking District, and the ice rink at Rockefeller Center, "and since," recalls Janet, "he had been wanting to paint Roseland, that's where we spent our first date dancing the night away." Ten years later they married and five or six years into that she shut down her business and then reopened it on the other end of Manhattan on Mott Street. Then as fate would have it, just around the time of 9/11 when they had been looking around for a summer home in Rhode Island, they found a nineteenth-century beauty on a quiet side street in Newport and decided to move in full-time. That's the house I saw digging through my piles of *World of Interiors* (February 2016) that continued Janet's story. Boom! I was smitten again.

It had been years since we had been in touch, (I thought it was probably a visit to her Mott Street store, but she remembers a luncheon with a mutual friend.) No matter, I reached her through Instagram, and when I shared my love of her home pictured in that old volume marked with a ragged Post-it, she confessed they no longer lived there, having moved again to a cozier house in nearby Bristol. Turns out that is where she was brought up and the town where her mother still lives.

Previous page: A re-creation of a magazine photo I fell in love with many years ago of Janet's floral sundresses pinned to a clothesline today in her Bristol backyard.
Opposite: In the front sunroom, the wooden coffee table that looks like a stack of giant books is actually a trunk. The flowers in the tall skinny vase are fake, as are those on the charming straw hat made by legendary hatmaker Grevi. She had spied the little red trunk under the hat in a display at Bon Marché in Paris. She talked them into taking everything out of it so she could buy it.

"Essentially everything that was in that house is here," Janet told me when we eventually met up. "We sort of move our stuff from house to house." Bill finishes her sentence with— "We are nomads. We live in a space and then we move on bringing all our stuff with us. The curtains go up and then they come down." And that is why no matter where they live the ingredients that make a home a home come with them.

When asked why she loves flowers—real ones and fake ones and representations made of wood and ceramics (like those seen opposite), and floral prints on dresses and kimonos, and on pillows, wallpaper and painted on plates, on books, bags, bedspreads, and even blooming from slippers—Janet smiles and hints to its origin.

"I had an Italian grandfather who was from Perugia, an Italian immigrant. He had a garden in the back of his house. He was an incredible chef. He made wine. He lived in Italy in his head and heart and that had a profound influence on me." His daughter, my mother who is 99 lives in the same house that he had always lived in not far from here." Which is why after Covid struck they started looking for a place nearby. And the one they found, built as a summer cottage in 1928, "spoke to us the minute we saw it," says Janet. "It's near the water. It's close to my mother and a lot of our friends in Newport. And though it's smaller (2,500 square feet vs. the 4,500 square feet of their Newport home) they've each found studios nearby to pursue their work independently, and plenty of room in the house itself for all the things they've lived with and loved for so many years.

And while she thanks her grandfather for that first garden that inspired the dream garden in her head and all the things that dream has touched, she also thanks the inspiration of all those summers in Nantucket, going back to when she opened her first boutique there in the eighties. "It was such a special time because I was young and everything was fresh, and charming and always fun." And though it would seem Janet and Bill have finally found a place to rest and relish the things they have collected, created, and curated together Janet reminds us—"There's a nomadic aspect to us—there really is, and who know where we'll go from here?" she asks. Wherever that might be—London or perhaps Italy (remembering her grandfather's roots) "One thing is for certain," Janet insists, "there will be a garden."

Previous pages: Some people don't "live" in their living rooms, but this is not the case with Janet and Bill and their daughter, Jasmine. Guess what hangs over the mantel that faces all those comfy-looking sofas—a big wide-screen TV, of course! The other centerpiece of the room is a colorful abstract rug, part of a collection Bill designed for Christopher Farr. They would never shorten the sumptuous length of the Pierre Frey curtains that have hung in several of their homes. Instead, they just tie them up in stylish knots.

Opposite: A garden of Janet's delights lined up on a bamboo stick chest. The wooden flowerpots on either end were handcrafted by Stephen Lirakis, the legendary sailor of America's Cup fame in Newport.

In the dining room hovering overhead like a magnificent, winged spacecraft is a flamboyant brass chandelier created by French metal-smith artist Bernard Sabatier. It almost appears as if Bill's abstract oval painting over the mantel is in its clutches! The hefty American Gothic Revival table is surrounded by a foursome of Empire chairs with cushions made from one-of-a-kind needlepoint pieces she found at the Paris flea market.

When Janet Russo met Bill Jacklin it was an opposites attract kind of thing, which is what this tableau of his painting (Road with Shadows) and her red Chinese chest, another thrift shop find, demonstrates perfectly. The bowl was a gift from Bill's sister, and the two floral ceramics on either side are by her multi talented friend Bernadette Likaris, whose brother created the chandelier that hangs in this same room.

The bookshelf they built behind the staircase up to the second floor is, "totally inconvenient!" according to Janet. "But," she laments, "there was nowhere else to put it." With so many books, in the end it was ideal. The gallery of plates, platters and trays (some from England and Vietnam) on the egg-yolk yellow wall have a Bloomsbury feel. On the other end is a Mexican gilded mirror representing the Sacred Heart of Jesus. And at the other end of the international lineup of five colorful suspects painted on the tin cups is a feathered cap that I mistook as a turtle.

162

*While it looks to be the dressing table of a an old Hollywood movie
star, Janet's chinoiserie dressing table was actually found in a beautiful old home in Newport purchased by a good friend in the sixties.
It was the romantic centerpiece of a bathroom decorated with hand
painted chinoiserie wallpaper. Her friend unfortunately had to leave
it behind when she moved to—of all places—Los Angeles—a perfect
destination for it. But happily Janet can feel like a star herself each
time she takes a seat.*

Janet's not sure if it's a duck or a goose, but whatever the species (I guess goose!), it is an artful creation made out of papier-mâché. She has three of them throughout the house. She crowned this one on the bedroom wall with a paper flower and accessorized it with some of her favorite bijoux.

Above Janet and Bill's carved-mahogany bed with pineapple posts are a pair of Bill's paintings (Stars and Sea at Night). Blooms abound on the bed with a flowery coverlet and one pillow that spells out LOVE and is next to a slightly obscured Babar. The elephant was was Jasmine's first gift, sent ahead to sit in her crib in Vietnam before Janet and Bill went to bring her home in 1998. On the wall near the door is Bill's Tree with Birds. And, of course, there's a vintage chandelier casting a romantic light on evenings spent in bed reading. Asked why a chandelier in the bedroom, Janet's response: "Why not?"

166

"There's nothing I can't live without."

Janet Russo

Opposite: Jasmine's pink chest of drawers was part of a furniture set that Janet discovered in the garden of the Nantucket house she bought in the late eighties. It had marinated there for a year and a half and faded to the most beautiful color. Recently repainted by Bill, the chest has now returned to its original shocking pink hue.

Clockwise from top left: A close-up of Babar, who was sent ahead to Vietnam to keep adopted daughter Jasmine company until Janet and Bill arrived to pick her up. "He is definitely a special member of the family," says Janet. A pair of cozy felt slippers made in Greece and brought back by Janet are evidence once again of her green thumb for growing a garden of flowery things. (No water needed!) When Janet told me that the impressionistic hand-painted shade in their bathroom was painted by Timothy Mawson, who founded a legendary gardening bookstore in New Preston, Connecticut, I realized he had written one of my favorite books, The Garden Room.

"We gutted the kitchen when we moved in," shares Janet, "and made it look like it had always been here." Lined with cupboards of dishes, teapots, fancy glass dessert bowls, cups and saucers, and stacks of plates that have traveled with them from home to home it feels familiar and warm. The sunny yellow of the walls adds to the coziness as does the sunlight pouring in through three tall windows above the sink. A hallmark of previous kitchens is the view over the sink framed by Janet's colorful collection of postcards and the embroidered curtain valance plucked from a flea market table in Florence. The red chandelier used to be white when it hung in a former kitchen, and the growing collection of wooden cutting boards are from all over. The skinny shelf beneath the windows seems like a must-have feature as a home to a chorus line of whimsical objects with no culinary purpose, except to distract and delight the eye of the person appointed to boring dishwashing duty.

Many of Janet's postcards were collected over the years from all over—from the charming shops of John Derian in Provincetown, Massachusetts, New York City, and even The Royal Academy of Arts where Bill Jacklin's work is well-known. His 2023 survey exhibition Towards the Light *was at the Marlborough Gallery in London.*

Clockwise from top left: No matter the season, a wallpaper of giant blooming flowers and fruits by Nathalie Lété, guarantees a kitchen garden always in bloom. Janet poses in front of a large painting of Lake Como by Bill, a place they used to visit a lot before it became so popular. She feels commingling his artwork with her collections has brought a rare sophistication to their home. Janet's collection of vintage floral fabrics were the inspiration for many of the romantic print dresses that were the signature of her line simply called Janet Russo. The little ceramic pot of red roses is an Italian piece.

Opposite: Janet and Bill on a visit to Bali, spotted unusual light fixtures that looked like upside-down painted canoes. Turns out they were worn by cows during the traditional Bali cow races. One now lights the marble-topped table in the center of their kitchen.

With a table like this on the front porch, Janet and Bill never have a problem seating extra guests at Thanksgiving (hopefully a warm one) or any impromptu celebratory gathering. In their last home, they had to remove window casings to bring it into the house. In this house, they decided not to fuss and leave it full-time on the porch. The mishmash of chairs provide plenty of seating for a meal, arts and crafts, or a good game of musical chairs.

Riki Larimer

LIVING
with
THE SOUND
OF MUSIC

The first things Riki Larimer bought in 1985 for her weathered gray summer getaway in the Hamptons two hours and some away from her busy life in New York City, were a century-old pair of wooden decoys. Since that time, they have perched on top of the wood-burning Franklin stove that warms up the house on that rare occasion (this is mostly a summer retreat) when the wind blows off the lake to bring the temperature down. Those poor ducks with their backs to that large luminous body of water just out of reach have only dreamed of what it might be like to float beyond their landlocked home. But after so much time one assumes they have resigned themselves to their role as guardians of Riki's sunny space—her home away from home.

After Riki and her husband Bob, holidayed for nine years in their getaway home in Puerto Vallarta, Mexico, they decided it was time for a change. After they sold it, they enjoyed a few years as summer nomads. That was until they discovered a cozy, rather spartan one-bedroom cottage in the Hamptons. Its saving grace was the spectacular shoreline location a stone's throw from a large lake. Over the years, they added another floor, a wing, and Bob, not only a talented musician, and lyricist, but an avid gardener, turned the property around the house into a little flowering paradise. It became for them a precious refuge not only from their creative work lives not just for themselves, but for their family and friends. When Bob passed away ten years ago, Riki found great solace spending time there with all the things she and Bob had collected over the years—the beautiful ebony upright piano(page 176) with a painting of dancing black-and-white spectator shoes above it. "That's Bob's piano," says Riki. "The first time I saw him, when I walked into his office, he was at that piano playing—writing a jingle for some advertising client." The painting above it by her good friend, artist Susan Zises, (see her story on page 104) was inspired by Gene Kelly and Donald O'Connor in *Singing In the Rain*. "It was the first movie I ever saw," recalls Riki, wistfully. "But now, I'm tap dancing myself," she laughs. Her lifetime love of James Cagney inspired her to produce a musical on his life, which played to raves in London and off-Broadway in Manhattan. "Music," she says, "has always been part of my life and in this house. There's always music playing when I'm here." And then as if on cue a song from Damn Yankees fills the room, this leads Riki (a die-hard Yankee fan) to her cozy entrance hall where a bright blue chair, an original from old Yankee stadium resides among other Yankee memorabilia and plastic bats for guests who are encouraged to join in a rousing game of whiffle ball in the backyard. (Mind the geese!)

Besides those first arrivals of waterfowl and the ageless statue of the little girl (over a century old) that stands between them on top of the Franklin we spot another carved duck and a colorful toucan by Mexican artist Sergio Bustamente, souvenirs of Casa Riki, Riki and Bob's home in Puerto Vallarta. And what about that tall wooden giraffe standing near the dining room table about to nibble a tasty vine trailing from hanging plant nearby? Riki is quick to answer: "I went to Great Neck High School and our symbol was the giraffe. He always reminds me of those days."

Look around and a pair of whimsical Chagall prints on one wall face off with a bizarre matchstick piece of prison art on the opposite wall. That's the mix that Riki loves. Everything belongs as long as it has meaning and connects it to a person or experience she doesn't want to forget. The Chagalls belonged to her brother, Michael, (her only sibling), and the matchstick art originally belonged to me! She saw it hanging in my barn, and when I told her the story about how a prisoner saved his burnt matches to create a piece of art, she had to have it.

Opposite: First thing that welcomes you into the world of this die-hard Yankees fan the blue painted (slightly weathered) chair, an original seat from the old Yankee Stadium.
Previous page: Like a living piece of art, Riki's husband Bob's piano is paired with the painting of dancing shoes inspired by Gene Kelly and Donald O'Connor in Singing in the Rain, captured by artist Susan Zises.

WATER MILL

*Air, sun, and breezes from the lake are all that is needed to enjoy a rest-
ful moment in Riki's spacious and very personal living room. The blaz-
ing Franklin stove is original to the house. The pair of ancient decoys
on top were the first things she bought when she moved in. The framed
matchsticks to its left is prison art crafted by an unknown artist, a
prison inmate. "If only they knew how much I love it!" Riki exclaims.*

Clockwise from above: The sculpture of the little girl was already 100 years old when she became the guardian angel of their home 25 years ago. She holds a tag tied to a twig once inscribed with Riki's name—a souvenir from a dear friend's wedding. Riki takes a break under the pair of Chagalls that her brother bought in the sixties. When Riki and Bob started traveling to Asia for their business together they bought this Buddha in Hong Kong. Placed in their entrance way, he welcomes friends in a warm and peaceful way.

"I am
surrounded
by things that
bring back
memories of
people I love."

Riki Larimer

Left: Browsing through a local flea market Riki saw the rusty highway sign pointing to Wilmington, a place where she spent so many happy childhood days.
Above: Riki loves the affection in this painting by Louise Peabody of a young woman with her Australian Shepherd.

The first surprise when you climb the stairs is a petite painted table. Above it is a romantic portrait of posies. (Wait, where are we? This doesn't seem like Riki's style at all.) Riki explains: "All my childhood, my mother had that flower painting at the stop of the stairs. I never liked it. I still don't, but there it is at the top of my stairs."

Go a little further, through a bedroom doorway, and discover another out-of-kilter decorative non-Riki moment. It's her mother's antique desk. The story is she bought it when she married Riki's father in 1935. "I can see her paying her bills and her mortgage ($75 a month) and the happy day she wrote the final check! The seat of the chair was worn out, so she needlepointed it before she died. That has lots of meaning."

When Riki found these heavyweight roosters at a local Hamptons antique show, it was love at first sight. (I know, because I was with her!) When she got them to their new home in the tall grasses of her garden, she immediately christened them Carter and Howard, after me and my husband. She put little name necklaces so it was very clear who was who and that it was definitely me clucking out a piece of my mind to my feathered partner.

Robin Bell

LIVING
with
AUDACITY
& DOGS

When Robin Bell was a young model working in New York and Paris and other glamorous destinations, it wasn't unusual that her mind would wander and she would see in the mirror a very different girl, dressed not in a designer gown but in a fishing vest. And instead of high heels, she was in high waders ready to cast her line into the tranquil stream. All she ever wanted to do was fly fish. So, many years later, after she traded modeling for interior design and saw her two children take off on their own life adventures, she and her husband, Paul, decided to bring that shared passion to life. Their thought was to give up their cool downtown Manhattan loft for something more rustic like a cabin in Wyoming.

GOD BLESS AMERICA

I AM Proud to be An American

GIL SCHAFER
FOREWORD BY BUNNY WILLIAMS

Friends exclaimed, me included "Why move so far away from those that you love and love you so much?" And after much soul-searching, they agreed and redirected their compass from west to east. Eventually, they found a house to rent in Connecticut just a few hours' drive from the city. It was up a country road on a hill surrounded by woods and fields. The sound of streams running down from the freshwater lakes just a few miles from their front door was music to their ears.

Robin is very clear that the house they rented was not a "serious" house. "The idea of moving out West was about embracing a kind of casual life that was not fussy," says Robin. "I wanted the house to be a retreat from serious design and serious fussiness and be more whimsical and unstudied. I wanted it to have a feeling of a Hemingway retreat, a rustification that was a departure from what my work is." When they decided to buy, they started to search again. Then, they ended up realizing that they really loved the house they were in and bought it. "I made a workbook of all the things I thought should be done when we first moved in," Robin shares. "It was a very strategic plan and I prioritized what I thought had to be done, and very few of them did I end up doing. I think there's something to be said about waiting and getting to know your house. Getting to know your property and getting to know what your life is going to be like when you live there. Isn't a house a laboratory? I think anyone that feels that way falls in love with their house. I know I did," she adds with a smile.

The mirror Robin looks in today, (see on pages 192–193) is a gilded Federal antique once owned by Berry Tracy, a legendary collector and curator whose taste had always inspired her. The mirror is doubly precious to her: After victoriously claiming it an estate auction of his personal possessions, it was the survivor of a tragic fire in one of her former homes. When she decided to hang it against the rough river stonework of the huge rustic fireplace that was the centerpiece of their new home, Paul was horrified. "You can't put that beautiful delicate mirror on that rough stone fireplace," he exclaimed. And her response was "why not?" It's just the place she thought Berry would have chosen for it. Some people might see it as a mistake, but she sees it as a sign of audacity and confidence. Mistakes to her are the result of other people dictating what you should love. "When you're really sure in your gut about something," she says with conviction, "it's always right! You're going to be happy looking at it and living with it." Like the antique mirror on the rough stone fireplace—it works because it works for you.

Previous page: The gilded-tin fish caught in a little antique shop in Maine was meant for client, but it tugged at her fly-fishing heart. A favorite cabinet Robin raised her paddle for at a charity auction in St. Croix. That's Maybelline sprawled on the floor—one of Robin and Paul's pair of English Setters. "My dogs are my best accessories," laughs Robin.
Opposite: Clockwise from top left: Robin's love of fly-fishing was inspired by a beloved uncle and Joan Wulf, the first lady of fly-fishing. A landscape on a ceiling tile from her son Luke. A sculpture of stacked wood; Robin and Paul and their family of rescue dogs. A hand-painted wooden plaque.

When Robin decided to open up the kitchen to the living room (she was tired of being a prisoner preparing meals for family and friends having fun on the other side), by excavating a wall, her carpenter called to her and said, "I want to show you something!" She looked through a little opening and saw these river stones. She guessed it was the original fireplace that had been built over to create an "unmemorable" one clad with v-groove wood and brick. She knew in an instant they should take it down, but Paul was unsure. "Wasn't it covered up for a reason?" he offered. Guess who won? The next disagreement with Paul was over the placement of her cherished gilded Federal mirror on the rustic stone façade. Robin instinctively knew it was the legendary collector and curators perfectly imperfect mix, and something Berry Tracy, would have totally agreed with. Indeed, it was the marriage of elegance and rusticity. And it wasn't long before Paul applauded the choice!

Sometimes an older house (this one from the 1930s) can offer up unexpected gifts like the beautiful old rustic river-rock fireplace and hearth discovered by accident during an excavation to open up the kitchen, seen through the doorway on the right. Robin points out that they added the ceiling beams throughout "to give warmth and character to this very plain house."

"I love setting tables," says Robin. "It's a creative outlet." "I never plan them. They just happen organically." This one starts with an Indian cotton bedspread as a tablecloth. She has a great collection of them, along with old blankets and tartan throws for a cozier look, and African bark cloths for a particularly unique look. The moss centerpiece directed the choice of green-hued Pierre Frey dinner plates she found on eBay. The chargers have an earthy stone color and the straw mats add warmth. Her napkins are always cloth. "I collect those, too, she admits, and sometimes she prefers the way they look unironed—right out of the laundry. Her English brass candle holders housed in bubbly glass hurricane shades, travel everywhere with her. Some people would be horrified at the waterfalls of petrified wax drippings, but Robin sees them as reminders of "happy gatherings with people I love." "I like anything that shows life." If you look closely at the whimsical green wood-and-iron tasseled chandelier which lights the theatrical scene, you will spot a collection of tiny wishbones. They hang in memory of Lyn Furer, the amazing mother of Robin's childhood friend Pam Michaelchek. "She would hang them on her marvelous iron wagon wheel chandelier as reminders of great meals with family and friends and as a token of shared good luck for all of us," recalls Robin, wistfully.

Top left: To use as natural place cards, Robin collects leaves and presses them into a big book. "I like to have place cards because it's part of the setting, like a little stage set that makes each guest feel personally welcomed."
Bottom left: Robin always sets the table with her mother's silver bread baskets. "They have probably been with me the longest," she recollects. She thinks they were wedding presents for her mother and recalls their appearance in photos of her third birthday and later at her seventh.
Opposite: Robin's mahogany table was actually Paul's, bought when he was first married. They think it's a Sergio Rodriguez Brazilian table that came with the four chairs. Robin added the pair of Windsors at each end. "I like to mix," she says. It sits cozily in front of the stone fireplace.

Previous page: Robin sees the barnwood shelves in their sitting area (the vintage book sets are hers, the newer ones are Paul's) as a stage to display their special objects, like his letter from famed baseball player Pee Wee Reese and her little carved dachshund (see above). The Federal server is used to keep snacks and hors d'oeuvres safe from prowling dogs. The contemporary cocktail table stacked with books high and low is surrounded by vintage bamboo chairs. According to Robin, "The idea is to take everything and mix it up making things cozy and personal."

Opposite: In Robin's world every object has a story. A convention of mostly tiny creatures assembled on a living room table testifies boldly to this philosophy. Her love of squirrels, like the iron one that serves as a nutcracker, was inspired from an early age when she was "knocked out" to see this humble woodland creature represented on the majestic coat-of-arms of the dashing Nicholas Fouquet, finance minister to Louis XIV and creator of Vaux Le Vicomte. A crusty little frog watches a pair of iron mice scramble up the match box. The green-speckled hen is a cherished gift from her grandchildren, Nova and Ozzi. Their mother, Lake, created the glazed pottery dishes supporting the "magic" rock. A gilded bronze-and-crystal candy dish holds Robin's custom mix of green, yellow and chocolate M&Ms.

Clockwise from above: Bound books become a backdrop for precious objects. The cheeky carved dachshund inspired by the many real ones Robin has had in life, carries a little sign around his neck that reads "Arf, Arf, Mama". It was made by her daughter, Lake, when she was still in school. A South African clivia in bloom on the cocktail table. In the hallway just outside the Red Room, (on pages 200 and 201), a large gilded mirror from Robin's childhood layered with an empty Ogee frame looks over a disparate mix of objets and textures.

Clockwise from left: A stack of Robin's straw chapeaus adds a touch of summer to a wintry shelf of vintage volumes. What looks like a pink baseball glove is "a bright bright-as-as-all-get-out-pink, ridiculous chair," laughs Robin. No one was bidding on it at the auction where she spotted it and so she took it home for $10 and placed it immediately in The Red Room. "I like that no one would think it belongs there." Lighting the way just outside The Red Room, a Regency lantern painted a faux bamboo.

Opposite: "I love the stains on this table," Robin shares. She never puts a cloth on it or even place mats. "The wood is so pretty itself." The chairs on either side are all different and "kind of wonderfully weird," she says. During Covid she put another table at the end so she could separate and entertain two different families. She's kept it there to accommodate more guests or to use as a serving table. The lineup of candles protected by a varied collection of hurricane shades (her passion!) are all different shapes. Another passion is her collection of chocolate and candy molds—mostly rabbits. They used to appear only at Easter, but now they hang out all year because she can't bear to put them away.

Previous pages: When you open the doors to what Robin and Paul have romantically dubbed the Red Room, you are shocked by its size (likely a garage in an earlier life) and the big stone fireplace that takes up the whole wall at the end of the room (not seen). "It's our party room," says Robin, "and thanks to Paul, it's filled with at least fifteen speakers, so the sound of music for dancing or watching movies is incredible."

One of a pair of formal period chairs that came from the auction where Robin secured the American Federal mirror that used to hang in the home of her design hero—Berry Tracy (See Page 192 and 193). She upholstered it in, of all things—polka dots! "That's the fun of owning things and making them your own," she claims. "I love those kind of juxtapositions."

A bass Violin is on display like a beautiful sculpture in the corner of The Red Room. It's both a tribute not only to the music enjoyed there but to Robin's son, Luke, who would tow the large instrument to and from lessons during grade school. Robin confirms that it was her friend, the legendary cabaret singer and pianist Bobby Short of New York's famed Café Carlyle, that helped her son pick out the instrument and then invited him one night to perform with his band. Wow!

"The things I collect are like the punctuation marks of my home."

Robin Bell

Clockwise from the top left: The tiny elder of their dog family, Archie had the honor of a pied-à-terre of sorts in Robin and Paul's bedroom. A collection of heart-shaped boxes nestled together in Robin's upstairs workspace; An ancient, beautifully hand-embroidered pillow sits forlornly on a chair in the bedroom. Robin bought the pillow at least four decades ago. She knows it's falling apart, but, she says, "It's just one of those things I have to have with me."

Opposite: "First of all," Robin explains, "this is a bed I bought for myself before Paul and I were married. It was made in the West Indies in the nineteenth-century with pineapples carved into the posts. When we bought this house it just made it into the room. There were finials for the posts that didn't make it, and the foot rail is all chewed up thanks to a teething puppy that used to sleep at their feet. She has slept under it with a canopy, but she prefers it without—"I love seeing the bones of the bed."

Arnaldo Anaya-Lucca

LIVING
with
MY
CAMERA

What do you take with you after you've lived in the same apartment for twenty-one years? Ask Arnaldo Anaya-Lucca, who lived in a landmark building in the East Village of New York City for over two decades, and he answers without hesitation—"The picture of my mom and dad on their honeymoon." Then, ask him where he wanted to live when he first touched down in New York after a life with his family in Puerto Rico, one of five and a twin to boot, and he answers in a flash—"I always dreamt of having a loft." Why a loft? "Maybe being a photographer [his craft for almost thirty years] I love the daylight and the height and the space like a studio."

"I always liked contemporary things—like my Mom. We grew up in the seventies and she always loved that kind of architecture." So, clearly his mom would be very happy seeing the familiar family pictures, the light steaming in through the eight windows over nine feet tall, the beautiful wooden floors, the dazzling white walls in her son's new home on New York City's Lower East Side. Built in 1908, it was originally a school, PS 12, until the fifties. After it closed down (because of budgets cuts) it was abandoned for almost thirty years. In the eighties, developers scooped it up and renovated it. When he walked in the door "it was like coming home in a way," he says. "I saw the high ceilings and tall windows in a corner apartment on the top floor." It was the loft that he had dreamed of and in 2015 he moved in.

But there is something missing from Arnaldo's shifting home history, He spent thirteen winters in a Miami loft starting in 2022. About six years into his photography career, he found himself doing a lot of shoots in Florida, so he invested in a sunny loft with water views in Miami. But he soon became disenchanted with Miami's changing "party central," vibe as he describes it, and decided to give that up as well when he found his New York City loft.

So, now the big challenge was how to merge the furnishings and collections of two homes into one. "When I first lived in the East Village my apartment was all Mission furniture. When people sat down, they complained." A good friend told him point blank, "This is not working. Let's go shopping." Looking back on that moment makes Arnaldo laugh. He was very into fashion and was already forty so he let his friend pick out a sofa, leading him into a whole midcentury style change. "But, I loved it," he confesses. He loved the sofa—the lines, the wooden frame, its simplicity. From there he started building out a whole new sensibility: an Eames chair, an Arne Jacobsen coffee table, a look-alike Eames chaise lounge, an oversize leather mirror propped against the wall. It was a new, spare sensibility, but he filled it in with things that he had lived with from the past (remember the honeymoon portrait of his parents)and made it his own.

His travels for work take him away from the loft for weeks at a time, but when he returns the light streaming through those nine-foot-high windows illuminates the things that make it his personal sanctuary: his first camera, the wall of his friends artwork, a wooden rooster that reminds him of his childhood farm in the mountains, the honeymoon portrait of his mom and dad, and so much more and he knows he is home.

Previous page: Arnaldo's first Yashica camera, given to him by his parents when he was seventeen.
Opposite: When he first moved in and posted some images of his new space, his friend, artist Kerry Irvine, texted him "Arnie, you need some art." Arnaldo agreed and Kerry's two abstract compositions evolved into a gallery wall of art and photography by other friends. There is something gallery-like about the place, which is not surprising given the fact that that the artist in residence always has a camera in hand.

"If there was a fire, I'd grab the picture of my mom & dad on their honeymoon."

Arnaldo Anaya-Lucca

Clockwise from top left: Arnaldo holds his first camera, a Yashica given to him by parents on his seventeenth birthday; Arnaldo's precious photograph of his parents on their honeymoon. He loves the old-school look of the globe he picked up in a vintage shop for $20. It inspires him "to dream about new places to visit and find all the amazing places on earth I have already traveled to."

Opposite: On the wall is a work by Catalan artist Jordi Alcaraz. "I saw this piece at Art Basel in Miami and bought it on the spot," says Arnaldo. "I love how he punches old books and impales them with other things—almost like an installation. The rooster reminds him of good times from his childhood spent on the family's farm in the mountains.

Following pages: No matter the weather, Arnaldo's world is always filled with beautiful light thanks to pristine white walls and tall windows that wrap around his top floor loft.

Mary Randolph Carter

LIVING
with
MORE ROOM
FOR MY
STUFF

Howard loves to walk through Elm Glen Farm, our home away from home for almost forty years and count the paintings on the walls. "Aha!" he'll yell to me from another room, "I just counted 165, and that's just downstairs." I'm not surprised. Paintings are my passion. I've hunted them down at the flea markets on Portobello Road, Bermondsey, and Old Spitafields in London, at Les Puces in Paris, at the Rose Bowl in Pasadena, at all of New York City's pocket fleas that used to pop up in parking lots on the weekend—the one I miss the most is the Garage. And, of course, there's Brimfield, America's classic held three times a year in Massachusetts. I think of each painting as an original masterpiece. No posters or prints for me. I'd rather hang a landscape or a portrait found in an art school trash bin than a poster of the Mona Lisa. The exhibition seen on our living room wall at right is a perfect example of how I love to mix them all."

When we moved into Elm Glen Farm every wall was originally covered with wallpaper. It's not surprising as wallpaper was an easy way to camouflage aging plaster, discoloration, and cracks in old houses likes these. Never a fan of wallpaper, stripping it all off was project number one. Once the walls were cleaned up and coated in white the fun began. I've always felt white walls were the way to make everything in a room stand out—not only the artwork, but all the furnishings too. Floors, on the other hand, I love as is. Luckily, most of the floors at Elm Glen were original wide boards of pine (see pages 228 and 229). For the floors in the music room (opposite and following pages), I painted a bright school bus yellow. The three fireplace mantels, were plain jane white when we moved in. It wasn't long before I started to scrape away that boring top layer hoping to reveal more interesting layers underneath. Looking at the mantel in the music room, you would think that's exactly how I found it. Unfortunately, I didn't find anything worth saving underneath, so I decided to create what I had hoped to find using splatters of green and black paint.

Once we had Elm Glen Farm, I naively thought I could begin to transport a lot of my collections from our apartment in the city to our refuge in the country. (How silly of me!) Once I started to curate the walls with artworks, like the large three-dimensional bird at right, and fill the cupboards with my blessed family of Infant Jesus of Prague, and transform mantelpieces with forests of my miniature evergreens, well, of course, there was no room for my city stuff. And truth be told, how could I live without all that beloved clutter in both houses?

Of course, there were pieces and paintings we had lived with in the little house in a neighboring county we had rented for several years before the purchase of Elm Glen, but until we had removed all that challenging wallpaper, none of it seemed to fit. Once we had a clean slate of white walls, things from our former getaway began to find a place and astonishingly reinvented themselves in this new environment. For example the green-and-white gingham chair (following pages) had been covered in a dull mustard velvet when I purchased it for our former residence, but it required a happy gingham makeover so it could start a new life on the bright-yellow floor in Elm Glen's.

One big addition to our Elm Glen life was Howard's mother's baby grand piano. Its arrival motivated me to collect musically inspired artwork like the large portrait of a piano player over the music room mantel (we think he might be Hoagy Carmichael) and the painting of the mysterious woman in the red gown at her own baby grand over the green cupboard. Once it had a new found purpose, we happily rechristened it The Music Room, abandoning its former ignominious title "The Purposeless Room" bestowed by Howard, who constantly questioned its purpose.

Previous page: Our beautiful granddog, Cora, looking very patriotic on our living room sofa bedecked with vintage handmade American flags. Cora was rescued by our son, Carter, and his wife, Kaisa, years ago.

Opposite: The six-foot panel of an exotic feathered bird is constructed of pieces of painted wood. It's one of a pair I found many years ago at The Rhinebeck Antique show which is held annually at the Dutchess County Fairgrounds. The birchwood lamp shaded with green paper leaves is a bit of fire hazard, so I rarely turn it on.

"Everything I love
is connected to
someone special
in my life."

Mary Randolph Carter

Previous page: Once we shoehorned Howard's mother's baby grand piano into the corner of the front parlor we renamed it The Music Room. That became the inspiration for the portrait of the piano player over the mantel, who we think might be Hoagy Carmichael, and the mysterious woman in red at her own baby grand over the green cupboard. My favorite piece might be the little green table between the chairs signed by, or created for, someone name MOE!

Clockwise from top left: The background music of our family reverberates when Howard's fingers run across the ivories of his mother's piano. When guests arrive at the front door of Elm Glen, the message that greets them (before our hugs) is spelled out below their feet on a slightly tattered hooked rug—"Welcome Friends." Since my childhood I've been touched by the spirit of the Infant Jesus of Prague. Now I own more than three dozen, including this large ceramic version guarding a blessed family of them stored in the cupboard behind.

Opposite: While their big furry cousins are up to all kinds of mischief (knocking over our garbage cans and swiping down our bird feeders), these two little bears await the children who will enjoy them just as ours did.

During winter months we gather in this cozy room warmed by the large fireplace, shelves of vintage books, and furniture and floors camouflaged in the colors and patterns of the American Southwest.

Just inside the front door you can store your walking stick in what was once a concrete pipe, now romanced with painted swallows, and tip your hat hello to elk and a handmade flat decoy of a long-necked Canadian Goose.

What better place to display my collection of shell-encrusted vessels than in what was once a barnacle-covered corner shelf! A primitive hickory chair does double duty as a hatrack for a worn-out straw hat. On the wall is a trio of wildlife paintings: a catch of fish and a pair of wolf portraits brought back from Ireland for my father.

One of my first purchases after we moved into Elm Glen Farm, was the metal garden table in front of the fireplace. I picked it up at a yard sale in town for $10, and here it has sat for almost four decades. We love sitting around it for dinner on a wintry night in front of a crackling fire. When I bought it, I didn't even consider how perfect it was for those fireplace dinners. Made out of metal there is no danger of an errant spark to fly and catch it on fire. Every so often I dip a kitchen sponge in some blue paint and smear it over flaking paint and candlewax. I painted the mantelpiece a bright school bus yellow to brighten things up and draped a string of tiny pinecones across it for fun. The cherub above is made of some kind of synthetic material that looks like cement. Every Palm Sunday he's happy to relieve us of our palms brought home from mass. The quartet of unframed paintings surrounding him were chosen for their green palettes. Of the hundreds of paintings I have collected, the majestic purple mountain, called Round Top on the wall to the left is my favorite. I bought it when we first discovered this part of the world and rented a little house in an apple orchard with a view of a mountain that looked just like it. The giant books stacked on the little stool to its left are actually made of wood. When night falls, I the light red candles (actually screw them in as they're battery-operated) in the yellow chandelier The blue table is scattered with books, a candelabra of real wax candles, and a statue of a little girl made of clay. Through the doorway is what we call "The Room For All Seasons"—named for its walls crammed with winter, fall, spring, and summer landscapes. The one exception is the portrait of the man in the hat resting on the floor against a bookshelf filled with vintage cookbooks.

Above: The dining room corner cupboard, hosts a collection of carnival chalkware figurines—bluebirds (top shelf) flutter around a painted folk-art altar to some unknown saint and parrots below guard a trio of vintage painted wine decanters in the shape of Spanish ladies and matadors.

Left: A lavish topiary of ceramic fruit and vegetables adds a bit more crazy color to The Music Room. It was one of those things that stood out on a cluttered flea market table that I thought quite tacky and not my style, until I circled it again and again, and then for what reason I don't know, just couldn't resist and bought it home to make me smile.

Right: A romantic chalkware ballet shoe in an en pointe position displayed appropriately on our baby grand piano. Was it perhaps inspired by that famous movie 1948 movie The Red Shoes *based on the romantic fairy tale by Hans Christian Anderson? Absolutely!*

Below: Ever since I placed this little faded red-and-white bench on the wall of our dining room it has never offered a seat to anyone—except the red-wood squirrel and the pair of dashing wine-bottled soldiers with red felt hats. The un-framed paintings lined up on the seat form a mini gallery. Underneath are stacks of gardening books and a wooden bowl of braided strings. Through the door at right is a peek into our kitchen.

Following pages: The ceiling of our original kitchen was right under the center beam where the steel orb is hanging. When we finally decided to take it down and open the space to more light, we had no idea it would expose beautiful wood beams and pegs framing its perimeter. I'll never forget the first sight of that transformation! It was a risk that paid off.

Our home in the country is all about living in the seasons: snuggling up in front of one of our fireplaces in winter, watching the leaves float down from our ancient oak trees in the fall; looking forward to the first signs of spring when the daffodils unfurl their yellow blooms; listening to the steady rain that starts to fill our stream; and finally delighting in hot summer days with visiting grandchildren in search of cucumbers and tomatoes peeking out from under the leafy vines and stalks in our vegetable garden.

No matter the season, our kitchen (previous pages) is headquarters. First thing in the morning we plunk ourselves down at the marble-top island and sip big mugs of coffee. No matter the weather, the light streams in through a huge window set in the peak of the ceiling and a pair on either side of the stove. From there I can admire all the things that brighten this big, white space and recall their stories and why I hold them so dear. There are the open shelves of Nathalie Lété plates and a collection of polka-dotted pitchers, a theme that continues on the crockery holding silverware and wooden cooking implements. You can spot them again on the set of frosty tumblers on the counter next to a painted-glass vase of my prized dahlias. Balanced on either side of the beam that runs under the big window are two pieces of flag-celebratory art: on the left a portrait of me by my friend Daniela Kamiliotis and on the right a picket-painted flag, a gift from our son Sam. The serape-covered wingback chair at the far right, known as Howard's throne, was upholstered in a kind of fake blue velvet when I picked it out of a barn full of mismatched chairs decades ago. It wasn't long before it went through its first metamorphosis of orange-and-red striped serape fabric. A victim of a kitchen flood a couple of years back, I chose the vintage serape to bring it back. The painting behind it, a special commission by my brother Jimmie, was inspired by *Le Café* by Pierre Bonnard.

When the weather warms up, we sip our coffee on the patio (called the piazza) through the screen door off the kitchen or out on the porch(following pages). We doubled its size to make room for a round wicker table big enough to allow meals to be served alfresco.

Opposite: I took an old cupboard, painted it white, and hung it on the wall of the porch to house things I've hunted down from yard sales and flea markets over the years—from ceramic pineapples to patriotic goblets and handmade toy boats.
Following pages: Once we extended our porch to make room for outdoor dining, it was as if we were eating in the trees. On one visit to an antiques shops in Hudson, New York, we furnished it with a collection of vintage wicker. The fold-up wire Ikea chandelier over the table was a gift from my mother. When we're not sharing a meal, you might find Howard and me competing at his vintage checkerboard.

235

There was a knock at the front door, an immediate tip-off that this was someone who wasn't an Elm Glen Farm regular use to coming in through the kitchen door. And so, it was not surprising that the two young men standing there were not regulars, yet not total strangers to Elm Glen Farm. Their grandfather, an artist, who had lived just up the road, had been a good friend to the former owner of Elm Glen, and they had a tradition of sharing their personal paintings with each other. In cleaning out his possessions, they came across a painting of Elm Glen Farm (left), and had come to return it to the place it commemorated. Startled by their story and elated by the thoughtfulness of their gift, I invited them in, and we sat on the porch and traded stories about the farm they had known from their childhood. On the back of the canvas in pencil was written "Elm Glen Farm—View From The Meadow." There was no date, just the name of the artist Jack Baretto, Elm Glen Farm, Millerton. (And the tiny handwritten directive Not for Sale.) Today it hangs in in our hallway right near the front door where those two young messengers of its past brought it home. Of all the things that fill this house, this is the one that fills my heart the most.